Rosa Luxemburg: The Incendiary Spark

"This remarkable collection of essays on Rosa Luxemburg covers the full range of her thought—economic, political, and social—while brimming throughout with profound reflections on her contemporary importance for today's world."

—**Peter Hudis**, General Editor, *The Complete Works of Rosa Luxemburg*

"A marvellous and engaging collection of essays that approach Rosa Luxemburg's legacy with fresh eyes and illuminate its enduring relevance for the twenty-first century. Michael Löwy elegantly captures the rather neglected philosophical dimension of Luxemburg's writings by bringing Luxemburg's dialectical vision of praxis closer to her systemic critique of capitalist accumulation, colonialism, and imperialism and by reminding us of the urgent importance of the categorical imperative of internationalism in times of climate crisis."

—**Ankica Čakardić**, author, *Like a Clap of Thunder: Three Essays on Rosa Luxemburg*

"This book presents a kaleidoscopic overview of the many contributions by one of the great revolutionaries of the twentieth century. Drawing on decades of engagement with the thought of Rosa Luxemburg, Michael Löwy discusses the many different aspects of her work. The essays collected here contain valuable suggestions for a socialism that is revolutionary, insurgent, and democratic."

—**Alex de Jong**, codirector, International Institute of Research and Education, Amsterdam

"With originality and verve, *Rosa Luxemburg: The Incendiary Spark* provides a deft exploration of many facets of Rosa Luxemburg's awe-inspiring life and work. Both an excellent entry point and a sure-footed guide to the intricacies and pertinence of her achievement, this is a volume that showcases the kind of scholarship we have come to expect from the eloquent and knowledgeable Michael Lowy. His vivid and animated style brings to the topic both a fresh urgency and a lifetime of distilled research, all refracted through a sharp and often unsettling gaze that yields success on every imaginable front."

—**Alan Wald**, H. Chandler Davis Collegiate Professor Emeritus, University of Michigan

Rosa Luxemburg

The Incendiary Spark

Essays by Michael Löwy

Edited by Paul Le Blanc
with a foreword by Helen C. Scott

Haymarket Books
Chicago, Illinois

Published in 2024 by
Haymarket Books
P.O. Box 180165
Chicago, IL 60618
773-583-7884
www.haymarketbooks.org
info@haymarketbooks.org

ISBN: 978-1-64259-982-4

Distributed to the trade in the US through Consortium Book Sales and Distribution (www.cbsd.com) and internationally through Ingram Publisher Services International (www.ingramcontent.com).

This book was published with the generous support of Lannan Foundation, Wallace Action Fund, Marguerite Casey Foundation, and International Institute for Research and Education.

Special discounts are available for bulk purchases by organizations and institutions. Please email info@haymarketbooks.org for more information.

Cover design by Josh On.

Library of Congress Cataloging-in-Publication data is available.

Entered into digital printing February 2024.

Contents

Foreword

Helen C. Scott

Rosa Luxemburg's life was bookended by revolution: she was born in 1871, the year of the Paris Commune, and was murdered in January 1919 by forces hostile to the revolutionary wave sweeping Germany and the globe. Born in Russian-occupied Poland, she spent most of her life in Germany, which was home to the largest party in the Second International—an impressive global network of Marxist organizations—the Social Democratic Party of Germany (SPD). She was one of the leading revolutionaries who broke with the mainstream of the International to oppose World War I, and she was one of the founders of the Communist Party of Germany (KPD). Luxemburg came of age in a tumultuous era that saw the growth and prominence of mass global working-class movements and profound challenges to both the reactionary old order and vicious new capitalism. This era came closer to achieving world socialism than any other before or since, and Luxemburg both was shaped by and contributed to the ambient spirit of possibility and transformation. While her life was brutally cut short, the written record of her experience as a revolutionary provides a bridge between then and now.

As with any significant public figure, we may glean much about Luxemburg from her friends and foes. She was loathed by the ruling class of her day, who labeled her a fanatic, accused her of treason, and incarcerated her for long stretches of time. This was in equal measure because she was a leading representative of a rising working-class movement that posed a threat to the social order, and because she was the quintessential outsider—Polish, Jewish, a woman, disabled—who refused to "stay in her place." In the routine attacks leveled against her, class invective was peppered with appallingly misogynist, xenophobic, antisemitic, and ableist slurs.[1]

She was also targeted by those on the left who were hostile to revolutionaries. In 1919 former comrades in the SPD sided with the ruling class, turned against the revolutionary masses, and ultimately had Luxemburg and countless other socialists murdered. In the ensuing century those advocating "socialism from above" have variously denounced, maligned, and distorted her record. This has been the case for Stalinism (under which model a powerful ruler delivers liberation on behalf of the people) and for the electoralism of Social Democracy (captured by Michael Löwy as "the illusion according to which parliament is the central axis of social life and the motive force of world history").[2]

Conversely, Luxemburg won deep respect and affection from workers and oppressed groups throughout and after her political life. In one of her first assignments as an organizer for the SPD, Luxemburg agitated among Polish miners in Upper Silesia. Her biographer Paul Frölich reports that while this was not an easy audience, Luxemburg won them over and they "brought flowers to her and did not want to let her go again."[3] Years later, on release from a long stay in prison for her antiwar activity, Luxemburg was greeted by working-class women party members in "overwhelming numbers" who showered her with gifts.[4] Successive generations of people and movements seeking fundamental social change and justice have looked to Luxemburg as a source of inspiration and political guidance. She continues to be recognized by antiwar, environmental, and social justice activists who gather to mark the anniversary of her death each year in Berlin. This reputation has been particularly strong in the colonized world because, as Löwy puts it, "[s]he adopted the viewpoint of the victims of capitalist modernization."[5]

Löwy makes it clear that he is among the latter group, a proud partisan for Luxemburg and all she stood for. This does not mean that his commentary is uncritical: he scrutinizes assumptions and omissions and takes issue with certain positions, in keeping with his recognition that Marxism is not a static dogma but self-critical and mobile. But he is interested in identifying her most important and lasting contributions, particularly her systemic critiques of imperialism and militarism; penetrating analyses of the accumulation of capital (the brutal processes of dispossession that have accompanied capitalist development at every stage); deep commitment to democracy; groundbreaking consideration of the mass strike as a central revolutionary tool for workers; dialectical understanding of the bourgeois state; and grasp of revolution as a process rather than an event. His finding is that Luxemburg is an essential point of reference for anyone engaged in emancipatory projects today.

Describing her thinking as "reflection in movement, which enriches itself with historical experience,"[6] Löwy emphasizes Luxemburg's intertwined theoretical and practical contributions, bringing us a vivid portrait of what Luxemburg called the "living political school" of revolutionary struggle. Engaging with the debates and conflicts of her and our moments, Löwy illuminates Luxemburg's commitment to revolutionary self-emancipation and explains her continuing relevance for the twenty-first century. Luxemburg looked to the mass activity of ordinary people as the source of hope for positive change. People across the world are seeking alternatives to a capitalist barbarism that patently threatens humanity and the planet we inhabit, while establishment political answers are less convincing than ever. As Löwy demonstrates in these essays, we have much to learn from Luxemburg's vital tradition of "socialism that is both authentically revolutionary and radically democratic."[7]

September 2022

Preface to the French Edition (2019)

This book is not a systematic study of Rosa Luxemburg's oeuvre, much less an intellectual biography. Many works have already undertaken such an objective, of which the best in my opinion remains the work of Paul Frölich, published in German in 1939 (during the author's exile), and its 1965 French translation published by François Maspero in the "Socialist Library" collection and overseen by Georges Haupt.

More modestly, the present work is a collection of essays that attempt to approach certain aspects of Luxemburg's beliefs, whether well known, unknown, or poorly understood, with the intention of looking at them with fresh eyes. Several of my articles concern the philosophical dimension of her writings. To be clear, the founder of the Spartacus League (*Spartakusbund*) never formally studied philosophy; Luxemburg's doctorate was, rather, in economics. Philosophy, however, is too important to be left solely to "specialists," whether certified or not. It must be noted as well that some of the most important Marxists of the twentieth century, such as Antonio Gramsci, were not professional philosophers either . . . I nevertheless believe that Rosa Luxemburg's oeuvre makes a unique and precious contribution to theory of history, political philosophy, and Marxist epistemology.

I have no intention of hiding my sympathy, admiration, and affinity for the ideas of Rosa Luxemburg. This does not preclude me from approaching her views with a critical eye, however. For example, in the afterword to the anthology *Marxists and the National Question, 1848–1914* (coedited in 1974 with Georges Haupt and Claudie Weill), I have demonstrated a clear disagreement with her refusal to endorse the slogan for national self-determination. Likewise, in certain of the articles in the present collection, I question her "pre-1914" vision of the inevitable collapse (*Zusammenbruch*) of capitalism. One should also add that despite her ecological sensibilities and her empathy for the suffering of animals, the question of the environment as a global political problem appears nowhere in her writings, but nor for that matter does it appear in those of other Marxists of her day. Nevertheless, I am convinced that any revival of Marxism in our times requires a rediscovery of Rosa Luxemburg: in envisioning the present and future of Marxism, her ideas are in many respects not simply important but indispensable. I endeavor in the following texts therefore to underscore the value, coherence, loftiness of vision, and timeliness of her writings, not only on socialism, democracy, and imperialism, but also on colonized peoples and the bifurcations of history as well as the dialectic between theory and practice or between science and social engagement. Future generations of socialists/communists will no doubt discover still other aspects in the cultural treasure of her oeuvre.

A few personal remarks for those who may be interested: I discovered the writings of Rosa Luxemburg in Brazil at the age of sixteen, when a friend gave me Brazilian translations of *Reform and Revolution* and *The Russian Revolution*. Not long afterward, during a trip to France, I obtained pamphlets published by Editions Spartacus. Finally, my mother had a collection of some of her letters from prison, which came out in Berlin during the 1920s. This was, in the words of Walter Benjamin, a "profane illumination" and the beginning of a passion for the figure, her history, her profoundly human character, her political intransigence, her martyrdom, and especially her thinking, at once revolutionary, insurgent, and democratic. I became and remain—all these decades later—a kind of "Luxemburgist," even if her constantly evolving ideas resist becoming a closed, fixed doctrine. As a young man, I was part of a small—nay, tiny (fifteen members on a good day)—Brazilian political organization, the Independent Socialist League, whose only historical, theoretical, and political reference was Rosa Luxemburg. Among its founders was a courageous veteran, Hermínio Sachetta, a former leader of the Brazilian Communist Party (PCB) and later of the Revolutionary Socialist Party (Fourth International), as well as two young Marxist Jewish intellectuals who taught me a great deal, Paul Singer and Mauricio Tragtenberg.

When I left Brazil for Paris in 1961 to begin my doctoral dissertation, *Young Marx's Theory of Revolution*, I worked with Lucien Goldmann, who was himself an admirer, if from afar, of the author of *Junius*. Even then, my conscious and deliberate objective was to offer a "Luxemburgist" reading of Marx, one that would put front and center the concept of the revolutionary self-emancipation of the proletariat. During the 1970s, I continued my research in collaboration with another admirer of "Rosa" (as she was known in our circle): the internationalist historian Georges Haupt. Works that I published on Luxemburg in the following decades were unequal in terms of their interest, originality, and scientific or political quality. I have selected for this collection those which struck me as timely, whether they were among the oldest (which is rare), or more recent (which encompass the majority).

In the intervening decades, I have added—with joyous promiscuity—many other names to my personal pantheon: Georg Lukács, Lucien Goldmann, Che Guevara, Leon Trotsky, André Breton, Franz Kafka, Ernst Bloch, Walter Benjamin, José Carlos Mariátegui. But the little Polish-German Jewish revolutionary who walked with a limp but who stood tall, who was both tender and audacious, brilliant and fearless, remains the brightest star in my constellation.

Translated by Lynne Sunderman

Addendum for the US Edition (2024)

A few words on the reception of Rosa Luxemburg in the United States in the postwar period.

In fact, this reception did not really start until the 1960s. Certainly, dissidents of Trotskyism, around Max Shachtman and Hal Draper, or Raya Dunayevskaya, mention Rosa Luxemburg in their postwar writings; Draper, in his influential essay *The Two Souls of Socialism* (1960), dedicates a few pages to her, as a representative figure of the current of "socialism from below." But the first important text on her is probably an article by Hannah Arendt, published in 1966 in the prestigious *New York Review of Books* as a review of the biography by J. P. Nettl, which was published in England. It is a very beautiful piece of writing that pays tribute to Luxemburg's foresight and denounces the responsibility of the German Social Democratic government for her assassination by the Freikorps. Arendt also examines her criticism of Lenin in the pamphlet written in prison on the Russian Revolution, but there she distinguishes, very explicitly, Vladimir Ilyich from his successor (Stalin). Curiously, she insists on the proximity between Luxemburg and Bernstein, despite their polemic—a very problematic assumption . . . The article did not have much impact on the North American Left of the time, which kept its distance from Hannah Arendt. It had a late legacy in a 1994 publication: Andrea Nye's *Philosophia: The Thought of Rosa Luxemburg, Simone Weil, and Hannah Arendt*, published in New York by Routledge.

Interestingly, the first major collection of her writings was published in 1970 by Mary-Alice Waters, a young leader of the Socialist Workers Party (SWP), the main North American Trotskyist party, by

Pathfinder Press: *Rosa Luxemburg Speaks*. In an extensive thirty-two-page introduction, Waters presents Luxemburg's work and life in a very positive but not uncritical way. In 1971, Dick Howard, at that time a young Marxist academic, published another collection: *Selected Political Writings of Rosa Luxemburg*, with the foremost left-wing North American publisher, Monthly Review Press, which also published an edition of Frölich's Luxemburg biography (1972). Can these publications be seen as a kind of late effect of the rise of the "New Left" in the 1960s? Perhaps, but the publishers, Pathfinder and Monthly Review, are rather representative of the "old" Marxist Left—admittedly, one was autonomous from the political parties and the other assigned an editor from the new generation of the Trotskyist movement.

In 1980 appeared what is perhaps the first book dedicated to Rosa Luxemburg by an American author, Stephen Bronner—close to the American socialist current represented by Michael Harrington—*Rosa Luxemburg: A Revolutionary for Our Times*; it is perhaps no coincidence that this first edition was published in London by Pluto Press. It was only in 1987 that the book would be published in the United States, in New York (Columbia University Press).

In the meantime, in 1982, another work appeared by an American author, Raya Dunayevskaya: *Rosa Luxemburg, Women's Liberation and Marx's Philosophy of Revolution* published by Humanities Press. A secretary of Leon Trotsky in her youth, after having belonged to various Trotskyist organizations, Dunayevskaya separated from this movement, defining the USSR as "state capitalism," and organizing a small autonomous political current, which defined itself as Marxist humanism. In her book she expresses her agreement with Luxemburg's judgment on the role of the spontaneous movement of the masses in the great strikes of 1905 in Russia; but she insists on her solidarity with the October Revolution, and she minimizes the criticism of the Bolsheviks in Luxemburg's 1918 pamphlet on the Russian Revolution.

Paul Le Blanc, an intellectual of the Trotskyist movement—expelled from the SWP, he joined Solidarity, created by former members of this party and others from the current founded by Hal Draper—in 1999 edited a collection of texts by and about Luxemburg, *Rosa Luxemburg, Reflections and Writings* (published in New York by Humanity Books). This volume includes four American authors: a 1985 lecture on Luxemburg by Raya Dunayevskaya; an excerpt from Andrea Nye's book on her feminism; a (critical) lecture by psychiatrist Claire Cohen; and an essay by Paul LeBlanc himself, who compares Luxemburg's conceptions of the party with those of Lenin, insisting on their convergences.

The publication of Rosa Luxemburg's writings in the United States took a new start in the 2000s, thanks in particular to the disciples of Raya Dunayevskaya, founders of the International Marxist-Humanist Organization. Two academics linked to this movement, Peter Hudis and Kevin Anderson, published a new collection in 2004, *The Rosa Luxemburg Reader*, once again with Monthly Review Press. Finally, in 2013, under the direction of Peter Hudis, William Pelz (a disciple of Hal Draper), and Paul Le Blanc, work on a fifteen-volume edition of the complete works of Rosa Luxemburg in English began: *The Complete Works of Rosa Luxemburg*, of which four volumes were published as of 2023. We can assume that this edition, published by Verso Books with the support of the Rosa Luxemburg Foundation in Berlin, is not unrelated to the recent revival of interest in socialism in the United States.

One could summarize this very partial assessment of the American reception of Rosa Luxemburg by noting that the Trotskyists and, above all, the dissidents of Trotskyism were the main—but not the only—people responsible for the diffusion of her writings and ideas in the United States. However, the important role in these publications of Monthly Review, which had no connection with this movement, should be underlined.

The main focus in this American reception of Rosa Luxemburg is on her political writings: she represents for her readers a democratic version of revolutionary socialism, in association with—or in some cases, instead of—Leon Trotsky. The discussion of her economic writings has remained marginal, up to the recent publication of the *Complete Works*, where they occupy an important place.

1. Rosa Luxemburg's Conception of "Socialism or Barbarism"

Is socialism the inevitable and necessary product of economically determined historical development, or is it only a moral choice, an ideal of Justice and Liberty? This "dilemma of impotence" between the fatalism of pure laws and the ethic of pure intentions arose within the German Social Democracy before 1914.[1] It was transcended—in the dialectical sense: *Aufhebung**—by Rosa Luxemburg, precisely through the expression, in the *Junius Pamphlet* of 1915, of the famous formulation "socialism or barbarism." In this sense, Paul Frölich was correct in writing that this brochure (whatever the errors and deficiencies criticized by Lenin) "is more than a historic document: it is the thread of Ariadne in the labyrinth of our times."[2] We will attempt to trace the methodological meaning of this phrase, a meaning which seems to us of essential importance for Marxist thought, but which has not always been sufficiently understood and evaluated.

For Bernstein, after his "revision" of Marxism in *The Premises of Socialism and the Tasks of Social Democracy* (1899), socialism no longer had an objective, material base in the contradictions of capitalism

---

* *Aufhebung* is a German word that the philosopher Hegel converted into an important category in his dialectics. As he pointed out, "this word has two meanings; it means to 'keep' or 'preserve' as well as to 'put a stop to' . . . " (G. W. F. Hegel, *Science of Logic*, quoted in Henri Lefebvre, *Dialectical Materialism* [London: Jonathan Cape, 1968], 35). It implies transcending or overcoming—but also preserving—a thought or reality in a higher synthesis. —Trans.

and in the class struggle. (In fact, the negation of these phenomena is exactly the central theme of his book.) He therefore sought another basis, which could only be ethical: the eternal moral principles, Right, Justice. It is in this sense that the concluding chapter of his book ("Kant without Cant") can be understood, where he opposes Kant to "materialism" and to the "scorn for the ideal" of official Social Democratic thought. These morals are quite evidently ahistorical and above social classes. For Bernstein, in effect, "the sublime ethics of Kant" is "at the base of actions eternally and universally human"; to seek there the expression of something so coarse and vulgar as the class interests of the exalted bourgeoisie was in his opinion simply "folly."[3]

In *Reform or Revolution* (1899) Rosa Luxemburg replied to the "father of revisionism" with a passionate and rigorous demonstration of the profoundly contradictory character of capitalist development. Socialism proceeded from economic necessity and by no means from the "principle of justice . . . the old war horse on which the reformers of the earth have rocked for ages."[4]

Yet, in the heat of the argument, Rosa didn't fully escape the temptation of "revolutionary fatalism": for example, insisting in the first section of the anti-Bernstein pamphlet that the anarchy of the capitalist system "leads *inevitably* to its ruin," that the collapse of the capitalist system is the *inevitable* result of its insurmountable contradictions, and that the class consciousness of the proletariat is only "the simple intellectual reflection of the growing contradictions of capitalism and of its *approaching* decline."[5] Most certainly, even in this document, which is her most "determinist" work, Rosa insists on the fact that the tactic of the Social Democracy in no way consisted of waiting for the development of the antagonisms, but of being "guided by the direction of this development, once it is ascertained, and inferring from this direction what consequences are necessary for the political struggle."[6] Yet the conscious intervention of the Social Democracy remains, in a certain sense, an "auxiliary" element, a "stimulant" to a process which is, in any case, objectively necessary and inevitable.

If "optimistic fatalism" is to Rosa Luxemburg in 1899 a temptation, for Karl Kautsky, on the contrary, it constitutes the central axis of his entire worldview. The thought for Kautsky is the product of a marvelously successful fusion between the illuminist metaphysic of progress, social Darwinist evolutionism and pseudo "orthodox Marxist" determinism.[7] This amalgam exercised a profound influence on German Social Democracy, making Kautsky the doctrinaire "pope" of the party and of the Second International. This was due not only to the undeniable talent of its author but also and especially to a certain historic conjuncture, at the end of the nineteenth and beginning of the twentieth centuries, a period in which the Social Democracy saw, with extraordinary regularity, an expansion of its adherents and its voting base.

Kautsky: Proletarian Revolution Is "Inevitable"

To Kautsky the problematic of revolutionary initiative tends to disappear, to the profit of the "bronze laws which determine the necessary transformation of society." In his most important book, *The Road to Power* (1909), he insists several times on the idea that the proletarian revolution is "irresistible" and "inevitable" and "as irresistible and inevitable as the unceasing development of capitalism," which leads to this amazing conclusion, in that remarkable and transparent phrase which sums up admirably his whole passive vision of history: "The socialist party is a revolutionary party, but not a revolution-making party. We know that it is just as little in our power to create this revolution as it is in the power of our opponents to prevent it. It is no part of our work to instigate a revolution or to prepare the way for it."[8]

It is especially beginning with the Russian Revolution of 1905 that Rosa Luxemburg began to differ politically with Kautsky and to criticize more and more the "rigid and fatalist" conception of Marxism which consists of "waiting with folded arms for the dialectic of history to bear us its ripe fruits."[9] From 1909 to 1913, her polemic with Kautsky on the mass strike crystallized the theoretical divergences latent within the orthodox Marxist current of the German Social Democracy. The principal object of Rosa's critique seemed to be the purely parliamentary character of the "strategy of attrition" extolled by Kautsky. But at a more profound level, it is the whole "passive radicalism" of Kautsky (in the words of Pannekoek), his pseudo-revolutionary fatalism which is put into question by Rosa. Faced with this waiting-theory, of which the obstinate belief in the "inevitable" electoral-parliamentary victory was one of the political manifestations, Rosa developed her strategy of the mass strike founded on the principle of conscious intervention: "The task of Social Democracy and of its leaders is not to be dragged by events, but to be consciously ahead of them, to have an overall view of the trend of events and to shorten the period of development by conscious action, and to accelerate its progress."[10]

The Role of the Proletariat

Still, before 1914 the break with Kautsky and with "socialist fatalism" wasn't complete. As the passage that we've cited shows, there was for Rosa a "course of evolution," of which it's only a question of "shortening" and "hastening." It was necessary for there to be the catastrophe of August 4, 1914, the shameful capitulation of the German Social Democracy to the Kaiser's war policy, the dislocation of the International, and the enrollment of the proletarian masses in that immense fratricidal massacre called "the First World War" in order to shake Rosa's deeprooted conviction in the necessary and "irresistible" corning of socialism. It was to overcome this trauma that Rosa Luxemburg wrote, in 1915, in the *Junius Brochure*, that remarkably *revolutionary* formula (in both the theoretical and political sense): "socialism or barbarism." That is to say: there is not *one* single "direction of development," one single "course of evolution," but several. And the role of the proletariat, led by its party, is not simply to "support" or to "shorten" or to "accelerate" the historical process, but to *decide* it:

> Man does not make history arbitrarily, but he makes history nevertheless. The final victory of the socialist proletariat . . .

will never be accomplished if the material conditions that have been built up by past development don't flash with the sparkling animation of the conscious will of the great popular masses. Frederick Engels once said: Capitalist society faces a dilemma, either an advance to socialism or a reversion to barbarism. . . . We stand today, as Frederick Engels prophesied more than a generation ago, before the awful proposition: either the triumph of imperialism and the destruction of all culture, and, as in ancient Rome, depopulation, desolation, degeneration, a vast cemetery; or, the victory of socialism, that is, the conscious struggle of the international proletariat against imperialism, against its methods, against war. This is the dilemma of world history, its inevitable choice, whose scales are trembling in the balance awaiting the decision of the proletariat.[11]

What is the origin in Marxist thought of the formula "socialism or barbarism"?

Marx, in the first sentence of the *Manifesto*, emphasizes that the class struggle has ended each time "either in a revolutionary reconstitution of society at large, or in the common ruin of the contending classes." It is probably this sentence which inspired Rosa Luxemburg when she spoke of the downfall of civilization in ancient Rome as preceding the return to barbarism. But there is not, to our knowledge, any indication in all the works of Marx that this alternative, which he presented in the *Manifesto* as the record of a past occurrence, might be for him valid also as a possibility for the future.

The Socialist Alternative

As for the phrase from Engels to which Rosa Luxemburg makes reference: it is evidently a passage from *Anti-Dühring* (published in 1877, which was almost forty years before Rosa was writing) that she attempted to reconstruct from memory (not having access in prison to her Marxist library). Here, then, is the text of Engels where for the first time the idea of socialism appears as an alternative in a great historic dilemma:

> [I]t is because both the productive forces created by the modern capitalist mode of production and also the system of distribution of goods established by it have come into burning contradiction with that mode of production itself, and in fact to such a degree that, if the whole of modern society is not to perish, a revolution of the mode of production and distribution must take place, a revolution which will put an end to all class divisions.[12]

The difference between the text of Rosa Luxemburg and that of Engels is evident: (1) Engels poses the problem above all in economic terms, Rosa in political terms. (2) Engels doesn't raise the question of the *social forces* which will be able to decide one solution or another: the whole text only sets the stage for forces and relations of production. Rosa on the other hand emphasizes that it is *the conscious intervention of the proletariat* which will be "tilting the balance" to one side or the other. (3) One frankly has the impression that the choice posed by Engels is rather *rhetorical*, that it is more a question of demonstrating ad absurdum the necessity of socialism rather than a real choice between socialism and the "perishing of modern society."

It seems therefore that, in the last analysis, it was *Rosa Luxemburg herself* who (while inspired by Engels) had, for the first time, explicitly posed socialism as being not the "inevitable" product of historical necessity, but as an objective historical *possibility*. In this sense, the phrase "socialism or barbarism" means that, in history *the dice aren't cast*, the "final victory" or the defeat of the proletariat are not decided in advance, by the "bronze laws" of economic determinism, but depend also on the conscious action, on the revolutionary will of the proletariat.

What is the meaning of "barbarism" in the Luxemburgian phrase? For Rosa, the world war itself was a sporadic form of the relapse into barbarism, the destruction of civilization. It is, to be sure, undeniable that for an entire generation, in Germany and in Europe, the forecast of Rosa revealed itself to be tragically correct: the failure of the *social-ist* revolution in 1919 led, in the final analysis, to the triumph of Nazi *barbarism* and the Second World War.

Socialism: One Alternative

However, in our view, the methodologically essential element in the phrase of the *Junius Pamphlet* is not that barbarism is offered as the only alternative to socialism, but the very principle of a historical choice, the very principle of "open" history, in which socialism is one possibility among others. The important, theoretically decisive element in the formula is not the "barbarism" but the "socialism or . . ."

Is it the case that Luxemburg reverted to Bernstein's position, to the abstract moralist conception of socialism as simply an ethical option, as a "pure" ideal whose sole foundation was the "will-o-the-wisp" called "the Eternal Principles of Justice"? In reality, the position of Rosa in 1915 is distinguished from, or rather diametrically opposed to, that of neo-Kantian revisionism by two crucial aspects:

1. Socialism is not for Rosa the ideal of "absolute" humanism and above the classes, but that of a class morality, of a proletarian humanism, of an ethic situated in the point of view of the revolutionary proletariat.
2. Above all, socialism is for Rosa an objective possibility, that is to say founded on reality itself, on the internal contradictions of capitalism, on the crises, and on the antagonism of class interests. There are socioeconomic conditions that determine, in the last instance, and in the long run, socialism as an objective possibility. It is these that mark the limits of the scope of what is possible: socialism is a real possibility at the end of the nineteenth century, but it was not in the sixteenth century, in the epoch of Thomas Müntzer. Men make their own history, but they make it within the framework of the given conditions.

This category of objective possibility is eminently dialectical. Hegel employs it to criticize Kant (real possibility as opposed to formal possibility), and Marx utilizes it in his doctoral thesis in order to distinguish between the philosophy of nature of Democritus and Epicurus: *"Abstract possibility . . . is the direct antipode of real possibility. The latter is restricted within sharp boundaries, as is the intellect; the former is unbounded, as is the imagination."* Real possibility seeks to prove the reality of its object; for abstract possibility it is necessary simply that the object be conceivable.[13]

It is therefore because there are objective contradictions in the capitalist system and because it corresponds to the objective interests of the proletariat that socialism is a real possibility. It is the infrastructure, the concrete historical conditions, that determine which possibilities are real; but the choice between diverse objective possibilities depends on the consciousness, on the will, and on the action of human beings.

The Conscious Intervention of the Masses

Revolutionary practice, the subjective factor, the conscious intervention of the masses guided by their vanguard now gain a whole other status in the theoretical system of Rosa: it is no longer a question of a secondary element which is able to "support" or "accelerate" the "irresistible" march of society. It is no longer a question of the rhythm but of the direction of the historical process. The "sparkling animation of the conscious will" is no longer a simple "auxiliary" factor but that which has the final word, that which is decisive.[14]

It is only now, in 1915, that the thought of Rosa becomes truly *coherent*. If one accepts the Kautskyan premise of the inevitability of socialism, it is difficult to escape a "waiting" and passive political logic. To the extent that Rosa only justified her theses on revolutionary intervention by the need for "acceleration" of that which was in any case inevitable, it was easy for Kautsky to denounce her strategy "rebellious impatience." The definitive methodological rupture between Rosa Luxemburg and Kautsky only produces itself in 1915, through the phrase "socialism or barbarism."[15]

War or Proletarian Revolution

A similar theoretical evolution can be found in Lenin and Trotsky: under the traumatic impact of the failure of the Second International, Lenin broke not only on the political level but also on the methodological level with Kautsky (of whom he had until then considered himself a disciple). He discovered in 1914–15 the Hegelian dialectic (the *Philosophical Notebooks*) and transcended the vulgarly evolutionist materialism of Kautsky and Plekhanov—a transcendence that constitutes the *methodological premise of the April Theses of 1917*.[16] As for Trotsky: in his early writings such as *Our Political Tasks* (1904), he proclaimed himself convinced not only of "the *inevitable* growth of the political party of the proletariat, but also of the *inevitable* victory of the ideas of *revolutionary* socialism within the Party."[17] This naive fatalist hope was to be cruelly disappointed in August 1914 . . . several months after the beginning of the world war, in a pamphlet published in Germany, *The War and the International* (1914)—and which was perhaps read by Rosa Luxemburg—Trotsky already posed the problem in entirely different terms: "the capitalist world is confronted with the following choice: either permanent war . . . or the proletarian revolution."[18] The methodological principle is the same as the Luxemburgian phrase, but the alternative is different, and no less realistic, in the light of the historical experience of the last fifty years (two world wars, two US wars in Asia, etc.).

In attributing to conscious will and to action the determining role in the decision of the historical process, Rosa Luxemburg in no way denied that this will and this action are conditioned by the entire previous historical development, by "the material conditions that have been built up by the past." It is a question though of recognizing in the subjective factor, in the sphere of consciousness, at the level of political intervention, their partial autonomy, their specificity, their "internal logic," and their proper efficacy.

Now, it appears to us that this understanding of the subjective factor, will and consciousness, is precisely one of the basic methodological principles of Lenin's theory of the party, the foundation of his polemic with the Economists and the Mensheviks. Thus, in spite of all the undeniable differences that existed even after 1915 between Rosa Luxemburg and Lenin, on the subject of the party/masses problematic there was a real rapprochement, as much in practice (constitution of the Spartacus League) as in theory: *The Junius Pamphlet* explicitly proclaims that the *revolutionary* intervention of the proletariat "seizes the helm of society" to take it "in the direction of Social Democracy." And, of course, it is not a question of the old Social Democratic International that had failed miserably in 1914 but of a "new workers' International, which will take into its own hands the leadership and coordination of the revolutionary class struggle against imperialism."[19] The significant evolution of the ideas of Rosa Luxemburg on this subject are revealed by a symptomatic fact: in a letter to Rosa in 1916, Karl Liebknecht criticized her concept of the International as "too mechanically centralist," with "too much 'discipline,' and too little spontaneity"—a distant and paradoxical echo of the criticisms that Rosa herself had made in another context, addressed to Lenin.[20]

Translated by Paul Le Blanc

2. The Spark Ignites in the Action

The Philosophy of Praxis
in the Thought of Rosa Luxemburg

In his presentation of Marx's Theses on Feuerbach (1845), which he published posthumously in 1888, Engels described them as "the first document in which is deposited the brilliant germ of the new world outlook." Indeed, in this little text Marx surpasses dialectically—the celebrated *Aufhebung*: negation/conservation/elevation—the preceding materialism and idealism, and formulates a new theory, which we could describe as the philosophy of praxis. While the French materialists of the eighteenth century insisted on the need to change material circumstances so that human beings could change, the German idealists affirmed that, thanks to the formation of a new consciousness of individuals, society would be changed.

Against these two unilateral perceptions, which both led to a dead end—and the search for a "Great Teacher" or Supreme Savior—Marx affirms in Thesis III: "The coincidence of the changing of circumstances and of human activity or self-change can be conceived and rationally understood only as *revolutionary practice*."[1] In other words: in revolutionary practice, in collective emancipatory action, the historical subject—the oppressed classes—transforms simultaneously both material circumstances and its own consciousness.

Marx returns to these problems in *The German Ideology* (1846), writing the following: "[T]his revolution is necessary, therefore, not only because the ruling class cannot be overthrown in any other way, but also because the class *overthrowing it* can only in a revolution succeed in ridding itself of all the muck of ages and become fitted to found society anew."[2]

That means that revolutionary self-emancipation is the only possible form of liberation: it is only by their own praxis, by their experience in action, that the oppressed classes can change their consciousness, at the same time as they subvert the power of capital. It is true that in later texts—for example, the celebrated 1859 preface to the *Critique of Political Economy*—we find a much more deterministic version, which regards the revolution as the inevitable result of the contradiction between the forces and relations of production; however, as his principal political writings attest, the principle of the self-emancipation of the workers continued to inspire his thought and his action.

It was Antonio Gramsci, in his *Prison Notebooks* in the 1930s, who used, for the first time, the expression "philosophy of praxis" to refer to Marxism. Some people claim that it was simply a trick to mislead his fascist jailers, who might be wary of any reference to Marx; but that does not explain why Gramsci chose this formula and not another, such as "rational dialectic" or "critical philosophy." In fact, with this expression he defines in a precise and coherent way what distinguishes Marxism as a specific worldview, and dissociates himself, in a radical fashion, from positivist and evolutionist readings of historical materialism.

Few Marxists of the twentieth century were closer to the spirit of this Marxist philosophy of praxis as Rosa Luxemburg. Admittedly, she did not write philosophical texts, and did not work out systematic theories; as Isabel Loureiro correctly observes, "[H]er ideas, dispersed in newspaper articles, pamphlets, speeches, letters . . . are much more immediate answers to the conjuncture than a logical and internally coherent theorization."[3] Nevertheless: the Marxian philosophy of praxis, which she interprets in an original and creative way, is the dominant current—in the electric sense of the word—of her work and her action as a revolutionary. But her thought is far from being static: it is reflection in movement, which enriches itself with historical experience. We will try to reconstitute the evolution of her thought through some examples.

It is true that her writings are traversed by a tension between historical determinism—the inevitability of the collapse of capitalism—and the voluntarism of emancipatory action. That applies in particular to her early works (before 1914). *Reform or Revolution* (1899), the book thanks to which she became known in the German and international workers' movement, is an obvious example of this ambivalence. Against Bernstein, she proclaims that the evolution of capitalism necessarily leads toward the collapse (*Zusammenbruch*) of the system, and that this collapse is the historical road that leads to the realization of socialism. This amounts in the final analysis to a socialist variant of the ideology of inevitable progress that has dominated Western thought since the Enlightenment. What saves her argument from a fatalistic economism is the revolutionary pedagogy of action: "[I]n the course of the long and stubborn struggles, the proletariat will acquire the degree of political maturity permitting it to obtain in time a definitive victory of the revolution."[4]

This dialectical conception of education through struggle is also one of the main axes of her polemic with Lenin in 1904: "The proletarian army is recruited and becomes aware of its objectives in the course of the struggle itself. The activity of the party organization, the growth of the proletarians' awareness of the objectives of the struggle and the struggle itself, are not different things separated chronologically and mechanically. They are only different aspects of the same struggle."[5]

Of course, recognizes Rosa Luxemburg, the class can be mistaken during this combat, but, in the final analysis, "[h]istorically, the errors committed by a truly revolutionary movement are infinitely more fruitful than the infallibility of the cleverest Central Committee." The self-emancipation of the oppressed implies the self-transformation of the revolutionary class through its practical experience; this, in its turn, produces not only consciousness—a traditional theme of Marxism—but also will:

> The international movement of the proletariat toward its complete emancipation is a process peculiar in the following respect. For the first time in the history of civilization, the

people are expressing their will consciously and in opposition to all ruling classes. . . . Now the mass can only acquire and strengthen this will in the course of day-to-day struggle against the existing social order—that is, within the limits of capitalist society.[6]

One could compare the vision of Lenin with that of Rosa Luxemburg with the following image: for Vladimir Ilyich, editor of the newspaper *Iskra*, the revolutionary spark is brought by the organized political vanguard, from the outside toward the interior of the spontaneous struggles of the proletariat; for the Jewish/Polish revolutionary, the spark of consciousness and revolutionary will ignite in the struggle, in the action of masses. It is true that her conception of the party as organic expression of the class corresponds more to the situation in Germany than to Russia or Poland, where already the question of the diversity of parties defining themselves as socialist was posed.

The revolutionary events of 1905 in the tsarist Russian Empire largely confirmed Rosa Luxemburg in her conviction that the process of the development of consciousness by the working masses resulted less from the educational activity—*Aufklärung*—of the party than from the experience of the direct and autonomous action of the workers:

The sudden general rising of the proletariat in January under the powerful impetus of the St. Petersburg events was outwardly a political act of the revolutionary declaration of war on absolutism. But this first general direct action reacted inwardly all the more powerfully as it for the first time awoke class feeling and class-consciousness in millions upon millions, as if by an electric shock. . . . Absolutism in Russia must be overthrown by the proletariat. But in order to be able to overthrow it, the proletariat requires a high degree of political education, of class-consciousness and organization. All these conditions cannot be fulfilled by pamphlets and leaflets, but only by the living political school, by the fight and in the fight, in the continuous course of the revolution.[7]

It is true that the polemical formula on "pamphlets and leaflets" seems to underestimate the importance of revolutionary theory in the process; besides, the political activity of Rosa Luxemburg, which consisted, to a considerable degree, of writing newspaper articles and pamphlets—not to mention her theoretical works in the field of political economy—shows, without any doubt, the decisive significance that she attached to theoretical work and to political polemics in the process of preparing the revolution.

In this famous pamphlet of 1906 on the mass strike, the Polish revolutionary still uses the traditional deterministic arguments: the revolution will take place "following the need for a natural law." But her concrete vision of the revolutionary process coincides with Marx's theory of revolution, as he presented it in *The German Ideology* (a work which she did not know, since it was published only after her death): revolutionary consciousness can only become generalized in the course of a "practical" movement; the "massive" transformation of the oppressed can be generalized only during the revolution itself.

The category of praxis—which is, for her as for Marx, the dialectical unity between the objective and the subjective, the mediation by which the class in itself becomes the class for itself—allows her to overcome the paralyzing and metaphysical dilemma of German Social Democracy, between the abstract moralism of Bernstein and the mechanical economism of Kautsky: whereas, for the former, the "subjective" transformation, moral and spiritual, of "human beings" is the condition for the advent of social justice, for the latter, it is the objective economic evolution that leads "inevitably" to socialism. That enables us to better understand why Rosa Luxemburg was opposed not only to the neo-Kantian revisionists but also, from 1905 onward, to the strategy of the passive "wait-and-see policy" defended by what was called the "orthodox center" of the party.

This same dialectical vision of praxis also enabled her to overcome the traditional dualism incarnated in the Erfurt Program of the SPD, between reforms, or the "minimum program," and the revolution, or "the final goal." By the strategy of the mass strike in Germany which she proposed in 1906—against the trade union bureaucracy—and in

1910—against Karl Kautsky—Rosa Luxemburg outlined a road that was capable of transforming economic struggles or the battle for universal suffrage into a general revolutionary movement.

Contrary to Lenin, who distinguished "trade-union consciousness" from "social democratic (socialist) consciousness," she suggested a distinction between *latent theoretical consciousness*, characteristic of the workers' movement during periods of domination of bourgeois parliamentarism, and *practical and active consciousness*, which emerges during the revolutionary process, when the masses themselves—and not only members of parliament and party leaders—appear on the political stage; it is thanks to this practical-active consciousness that the least organized and most backward layers can become, in a period of revolutionary struggle, the most radical element. From this premise flows her critique of those who base their political strategy on an exaggerated estimation of the role of organization in the class struggle—which is generally accompanied by an underestimation of the unorganized proletariat—forgetting the pedagogical role of revolutionary struggle: "Six months of a revolutionary period will complete the work of the training of these as yet unorganized masses, which ten years of public demonstrations and distribution of leaflets would be unable to do."[8]

Was Rosa Luxemburg therefore spontaneist? Not quite . . . In the pamphlet *The Mass Strike, the Political Party, and the Trade Unions* (1906) she insisted, referring to Germany, that the role of "the most enlightened, most class-conscious vanguard" is not to wait "in a fatalist fashion" until the spontaneous popular movement "falls from the clouds." On the contrary, the function of this vanguard is precisely to "*hasten (vorauseilen)* the development of things and endeavor to accelerate events."[9] She recognizes that the socialist party must take the political leadership of the mass strike, which consists of "informing the German proletariat of their *tactics* and *aims* in the period of coming struggle"; she goes so far as to proclaim that the socialist organization is the "vanguard of the entire body of the workers" and that "the political clarity, the strength, and the unity of the labor movement flow from this organization."[10]

It should be added that the Polish organization led by Rosa Luxemburg, the Social Democracy of the Kingdom of Poland and Lithuania (SDKPiL), clandestine and revolutionary, resembled the Bolshevik Party much more than it resembled German Social Democracy . . . Finally, an aspect that is often ignored must be taken into account: it concerns the attitude of Rosa Luxemburg toward the International (especially after 1914), which she conceived of as *a centralized and disciplined world party*. It is not the least of ironies that Karl Liebknecht, in a letter to Rosa Luxemburg, criticized her conception of the International as being "too mechanically centralized," with "too much 'discipline,' not enough spontaneity," considering the masses "too much as instruments of action, not as having their own will; as instruments of action desired by and decided on by the International, not as desiring and deciding themselves."[11]

Parallel to this activist voluntarism, the determinist (economic) optimism of the theory of *Zusammenbruch*, the collapse of capitalism, victim of its contradictions, does not disappear from her writings. On the contrary: it is at the very center of her great economic work, *The Accumulation of Capital* (1911). It was only after 1914, in the pamphlet *The Crisis of Social Democracy*, written in prison in 1915—and published in Switzerland in January 1916 under the pseudonym "Junius"—that this traditional vision of the socialist movement at the beginning of the century was to be transcended. This document, thanks to the expression "socialism or barbarism," marks a turning point in the history of Marxist thought. Curiously, the argument of Rosa Luxemburg starts by referring to the "objective laws of historical development"; she recognizes that the action of the proletariat "contributes to determining history" but seems to believe that it is only a question of accelerating or delaying the historical process. So far, nothing new!

But in the following lines she compares the victory of the proletariat to "a leap of humanity from the animal world into the realm of freedom," while adding: this leap will not be possible "until the development of complex material conditions strikes the incendiary spark [*zündende Funke*] of conscious will in the great mass." We find here the celebrated *Iskra*, the spark of revolutionary will that is able to make the dry powder of material conditions explode. But what does this *zündende Funke* produce? It is only thanks to a "long chain of violent tests of strength" that "[t]he international proletariat under the leadership of the Social Democrats will thereby learn to try to take its history (*Seine Geschichte*) into its own hands."[12] *In other words: it is in the course of practical experience that the spark of the revolutionary consciousness of the oppressed and exploited ignites.*

By introducing the expression "socialism or barbarism," "Junius" referred to the authority of Engels, in a writing going back "forty years"—undoubtedly a reference to *Anti-Dühring* (1878): "Friedrich Engels once said: 'Bourgeois society stands at the crossroads, either transition to socialism or regression into barbarism.'" In fact, what Engels wrote is quite different:

> [B]oth the productive forces created by the modern capitalist mode of production and also the system of distribution of goods established by it have come into burning contradiction with that mode of production itself, and in fact to such a degree that, if the whole of modern society is not to perish, a revolution of the mode of production and distribution must take place, a revolution which will put an end to all class divisions.[13]

The argument of Engels—primarily economic, and not political, like that of "Junius"—is rather rhetorical, a kind of reductio ad absurdum of the need for socialism, if we want to avoid the "destruction" of modern society—a vague formula: it is not easy to see exactly what it encompasses. In fact, it is Rosa Luxemburg who invented, in the strong sense of the word, the expression "socialism or barbarism," which was to have such a great impact in the course of the twentieth century. If she refers to Engels, it is perhaps to try to give more legitimacy to a fairly heterodox thesis. Obviously it was the world war, and the collapse of the international workers' movement in August 1914, that ended up by shaking her conviction of the inevitable victory of socialism.

In the following paragraphs "Junius" developed her innovating point of view:

Today, we face the choice exactly as Friedrich Engels foresaw it a generation ago: either the triumph of imperialism and the collapse of all civilization as in ancient Rome, depopulation, desolation, degeneration—a great cemetery. *Or* the victory of socialism, that means the conscious active struggle of the international proletariat against imperialism and its method of war. This is a dilemma of world history, an *either/or*; the scales are wavering before the decision of the class-conscious proletariat.[14]

We can discuss the significance of the concept of "barbarism": it is undoubtedly a question of a modern, "civilized" barbarism—thus the comparison with ancient Rome is not very relevant—and in this case what was affirmed in the Junius pamphlet turned out to be prophetic: German fascism, supreme demonstration of modern barbarism, could seize power thanks to the defeat of socialism. But what is most important in the formula "socialism or barbarism" is the term "or": what is involved is the recognition that history is an open process, that the future is not yet decided—by "the laws of history" or the economy—but depends, in the final analysis, on "subjective" factors: consciousness, decision, will, initiative, action, revolutionary praxis. It is true, as Isabel Loureiro underlines in her very fine book, that even in the Junius pamphlet—as in later texts of Rosa Luxemburg—we still find references to the inevitable collapse of capitalism, the "dialectic of history" and the "historical need for socialism."[15] But in the final analysis, the formula "socialism or barbarism" provides the foundations of another conception of the "dialectic of history," distinct from economic determinism and the illuminist ideology of inevitable progress.

We find again the philosophy of praxis in the middle of the polemic in 1918 on the Russian Revolution—another capital text written behind bars. The essential thread of this document is well known: on the one hand, support for the Bolsheviks, and their leaders, Lenin and Trotsky, who saved the honor of international socialism, by daring to make the October Revolution; on the other, a whole series of criticisms of which some—on the land question and the national question—are quite debatable, while others—the chapter on democracy—appear prophetic. What worries the Jew-ish/Polish/German revolutionary is above all the suppression, by the Bolsheviks, of democratic liberties—freedom of the press, of association, of assembly—which are precisely the guarantee of the political activity of the working masses; without them "the rule of the broad masses of the people is entirely unthinkable."

The gigantic tasks of the transition to socialism—"which the Bol-sheviks have undertaken with courage and determination"—cannot be carried out without "the most intensive political training of the masses and the accumulation of experience," which is not possible without democratic liberties. The construction of a new society is virgin terrain that poses "a thousand problems" that are unforeseen; however, "[o]nly experience is capable of correcting and opening new ways." Socialism is a historical product "born out of the school of its own experiences": the whole of the popular masses (*Volksmas-sen*) must take part in this experience, otherwise "socialism will be decreed from behind a few official desks by a dozen intellectuals." For the inevitable errors of the transition process the only remedy is revolutionary practice itself: "the only healing and purifying sun is the revolution itself and its renovating principle, the spiritual life, activity and initiative of the masses which is called into being by it and which takes the form of the broadest political freedom."[16]

This argument is much more important than the debate on the Constituent Assembly, on which the "Leninist" objections to the text of 1918 have been concentrated. Without democratic liberties, the revolutionary praxis of the masses, popular self-education through experience, the self-emancipation of the oppressed, and the exercise of power itself by the working class are impossible. Georg Lukács, in his important essay "The Marxism of Rosa Luxemburg" (January 1921), showed with great acuity how, thanks to the unity of theory and praxis—formulated by Marx in his *Theses on Feuerbach*—the great revolutionary had succeeded in overcoming the dilemma of the impotence of Social Democratic movements, "the dilemma created by the pure laws with their fatalism and by the ethics of pure intentions." What does this dialectical unity mean?

> We have seen that the proletariat as a class can only conquer
> and retain a hold on class consciousness and raise itself to the
> level of its—objectively-given—historic task through conflict
> and action. It is likewise true that the party and the individ
> ual fighter can only really take possession of their theory if
> they are able to bring this unity into their praxis.[17]

It is therefore surprising that, hardly one year later, Lukács wrote the essay—which would also appear in *History and Class Consciousness* (1923)—entitled "Critical Observations on Rosa Luxemburg's 'Critique of the Russian Revolution'" (January 1922), which rejects en bloc the whole of the dissenting comments of the founder of the Spartacus League, claiming that she "imagines the proletarian revolution as having the structural forms of bourgeois revolutions"[18]—a not very credible accusation, as Isabel Loureiro demonstrates.[19] How can we explain the difference, in tone and content, between the essay of January 1921 and that of January 1922? A rapid conversion to orthodox Leninism? Perhaps, but more probably the position of Lukács in relation to the debates within German Communism. Paul Levi, the principal leader of the KPD (Communist Party of Germany), had opposed the "March Action" of 1921, a failed attempt at a communist rising in Germany, supported with enthusiasm by Lukács (but criticized by Lenin . . .); expelled from the party, Paul Levi decided in 1922 to publish the manuscript of Rosa Luxemburg on the Russian Revolution, which the author had entrusted him with in 1918. The polemic of Lukács with this document is also, indirectly, a settling of accounts with Paul Levi.

In fact, the chapter on democracy of this document by Luxemburg is one of the most important texts of Marxism, of communism, of critical theory, and of the revolutionary thought of the twentieth century. It is difficult to imagine a refounding of socialism in the twenty-first century that does not take into account the arguments developed in these feverish pages. The most lucid representatives of

Leninism and Trotskyism, such as Ernest Mandel and Daniel Ben-
saïd, recognized that this 1918 criticism of Bolshevism, concerning
the question of democratic liberties, was in the final analysis justified. Of course, the democracy to which Rosa Luxemburg refers is
that exercised by the workers in a revolutionary process, and not the
"low intensity democracy" of bourgeois parliamentarism, in which
the important decisions are taken by bankers, contractors, soldiers
and technocrats, free from any popular control.

The *zündende Funke*, the incendiary spark of Rosa Luxemburg,
glowed one last time in December 1918, when she addressed the
Founding Congress of the KPD (Spartacus League).

Admittedly, we still find in this text references to "the law of the
necessary objective development of the socialist revolution," but it is
really about "the bitter experience" that the various forces of the workers' movement must go through before finding the revolutionary
road. The last words of this memorable speech are directly inspired
by the perspective of the self-emancipatory praxis of the oppressed:

> The masses must learn how to use power by using power.
> There is no other way to teach them. Fortunately, we have
> gone beyond the days when it was proposed to "educate" the
> proletariat socialistically. Marxists of Kautsky's school still
> believe in the existence of those vanished days. To educate the
> proletarian masses socialistically meant to deliver lectures to
> them, to circulate leaflets and pamphlets among them. No,
> the school of the socialist proletariat doesn't need all this.
> The workers will learn in the school of action [*zur Tat greifen*].

Here Rosa Luxemburg refers to a famous formula of Goethe, *Am
Anfang war die Tat!* At the beginning of all is not the Word but the
Action! In the words of the Marxist revolutionary: "Our motto is: In
the beginning was the act. And the act must be that the workers' and
soldiers' councils realize their mission and learn to become the sole
public power of the whole nation."[20]

A few days later, Rosa Luxemburg would be assassinated by the
paramilitary Freikorps—mobilized by the Social Democratic govern-

ment, under the authority of the Minister Gustav Noske, against the rising of the workers of Berlin.

. . .

Rosa Luxemburg was not infallible; she made mistakes, like any human being and any activist, and her ideas do not constitute a closed theoretical system, a dogmatic doctrine that could be applied to any place and any time. But undoubtedly her thought is an invaluable source of inspiration to try to dismantle the capitalist machine and think of radical alternatives. It is not an accident that it has become, in recent years, one of the most important references in the debate, in particular in Latin America, on a socialism of the twenty-first century, capable of going beyond the impasses of the experiences conducted in the name of socialism in the last century—both Social Democracy and Stalinism. Her conception of a socialism that is both revolutionary and democratic—in irreconcilable opposition to capitalism and imperialism—based on the self-emancipatory praxis of the workers, on self-education through experience and on the action of the great popular masses thus becomes strikingly topical. The socialism of the future will not be able to do without the light from this glowing spark.

Translated by International Viewpoint

3. The Hammer Blow of the Revolution

Rosa Luxemburg's defense of socialist democracy and her critique of the Bolsheviks in her pamphlet *The Russian Revolution* (1918) are well known. Less well known and often forgotten is her critique of bourgeois democracy, its limits, its contradictions, and its narrow and partial character. We propose to examine this critical line of thought in some of her political writings without any pretentions to completeness.

We begin this discussion with *Reform or Revolution* (1898), one of the foundational texts of modern revolutionary socialism, where this problem is taken up in a particularly intense way. This brilliant essay, the work of a young woman almost unknown at the time, is a unique synthesis of revolutionary passion and discursive rationality, filled with sparks of irony and lightning flashes of intuition. It remains, more than a century later, surprisingly contemporary.

But it is not without its defects, notably in its economic polemic with Eduard Bernstein, where she develops a sort of optimistic fatalism: the belief in the inevitability of the economic collapse (*Zusammenbruch*) of capitalism. It should be said in passing that this is an opinion that one finds even today among a number of Marxists who have announced that the current financial crisis of capitalism is "the last" and that it will bring about the definitive end of the system. It seems that Walter Benjamin, who knew the Great Crisis of 1929 and its results, formulated the most pertinent conclusion regarding this subject: "The experience of our generation: capitalism will not die a natural death."[1]

Nevertheless, in her discussion of democracy, Luxemburg dissociates herself from the facile optimism of the religion of democratic

Progress (with a capital "P")—the illusion of increasing democrati-
zation of the "civilized" societies—dominant in her era among both
liberals and socialists. This is also one of the strong points of her
argument. Furthermore, in her analysis of the liberal bourgeoisie,
one finds not a trace of economism: One sees here, in all of its force,
what Georg Lukács, in "The Marxism of Rosa Luxemburg," the opening essay of *History and Class Consciousness* (1923), designated as the
revolutionary principle in the terrain of method: the dialectical category of the totality.[2] Luxemburg discusses the issue of democracy
from the perspective of the historical totality in motion, where economy, society, class struggle, state, politics, and ideology are inseparable moments of a concrete process.

Dialectic of the Bourgeois State

Luxemburg's eminently dialectical approach to the bourgeois state
and its democratic forms permits her to avoid both the social-liberal
approach (Bernstein!) that denies its bourgeois character, as well
as that of a certain vulgar Marxism that does not take into account
the importance of democracy. Faithful to the Marxist theory of the
capitalist state, Luxemburg insists on its character as a "class state."
But she immediately replies, "This, too, like everything referring to
capitalist society, should not be understood in a rigorous absolute
manner, but dialectically." What does that mean? First, it means
that the state "without a doubt assumes functions of general interest in terms of social development," but at the same time, it only
does so "to the degree that the general interest in terms of social
development coincides with the interest of the dominant class." The
state's universality is thus severely limited and in a large degree ne-
gated by its class character.[3]

Another aspect of this dialectic is the contradiction between the
democratic form and the class content: "The formally democratic
forms are not democratic with regard to their content where class
interests dominate." But she does not limit herself to that finding,
which is a classic locus of Marxism; not only does she not disregard

the democratic form, but she shows that it can come into conflict with the bourgeois content: "This manifests itself in a tangible fashion in the fact that as soon as democracy shows the tendency to negate its class character and become transformed into an instrument of the real interests of the population, the democratic forms are sacrificed by the bourgeoisie and by its state representatives."[4] The history of the twentieth century is riddled with examples of this sort of "sacrifice," from the civil war in Spain to the coup d'état in Chile; these are not exceptions but the rule. Already in 1898 Luxemburg foresaw with impressive acuity what would happen throughout the next century.

Luxemburg opposes to the idyllic vision of history as uninterrupted "Progress," as the necessary evolution of humanity toward democracy, and above all to the myth of an intrinsic link between capitalism and democracy, a sober analysis, without any illusions, of the diversity of political regimes:

> The uninterrupted victory of democracy, which to revisionism as well as to bourgeois liberalism appears as a great fundamental law of human history and especially modern history, is shown upon closer examination to be a phantom. No absolute and general relation can be constructed between capitalist development and democracy. The political form of a given country is always the result of the composite of all the existing political factors, domestic as well as foreign. It admits within its limits all variations of scale from absolute monarchy to the democratic republic.[5]

What she could not foresee, of course, were authoritarian state forms even worse than monarchies: the fascist regimes and military dictatorships that would develop in the capitalist countries—in the center as well as in the periphery—throughout the twentieth century. But she has the merit of being one of the few in the workers' and socialist movements to challenge the ideology of Progress, which was common among bourgeois liberals and among a good part of the Left, and to demonstrate the complete compatibility of capitalism with radically antidemocratic political forms.

Bernstein, a convinced advocate of the ideology of Progress, believed in an irreversible evolution of modern societies toward more democracy and—why not?—toward socialism. Now, observes Rosa Luxemburg, "the state, that is to say the political organization, and the property relations, that is to say the legal organization of capitalism, become more and more capitalist, and not more and more socialist."[6] We see again the opposition between the Left and the Right in German Social Democracy corresponding to the antagonism between faith in ineluctable Progress of the "civilized" countries and the insistence on social revolution.

Not only is there no particular affinity between the bourgeoisie and democracy, but often there is a struggle. Yet it is in the struggle against this class that democratic advances take place: "In Belgium the conquest of universal suffrage by the labor movement was due to the weakness of the local militarism, and consequently to the special geographic and political situation and, above all, this 'piece of democracy' was obtained, not *by* the bourgeoisie, but *against* it."[7]

Is this just the case of Belgium, or is it rather a general historical tendency? Luxemburg seems to opt for the second hypothesis, considering that the only guarantee of democracy is the force of the workers' movement:

> The way out of this circle is simple: In view of that fact that bourgeois liberalism has given up the ghost from fear of the growing labor movement and its final aim, we conclude that the socialist labor movement is today the only support for democracy. We must conclude that the socialist movement is not bound to bourgeois democracy but that, on the contrary, the fate of democracy is bound up with the socialist movement. Democracy does not acquire greater chances of survival to the extent that the socialist movement renounces the struggle for its emancipation; on the contrary, democracy acquires greater chances of survival as the socialist movement becomes sufficiently strong to struggle against the reactionary consequences of world

politics and the bourgeois desertion of democracy. He who would strengthen democracy must also want to strengthen and not weaken the socialist movement. He who renounces the struggle for socialism renounces both the labor movement and democracy.[8]

In other words, democracy, in the eyes of Rosa Luxemburg, is an essential value that the socialist movement must save from its reactionary adversaries, among which one finds the bourgeoisie always ready to betray its democratic proclamations if its interests so demand. We have already seen several examples of this simple fact. What does the reference to the "reactionary consequences of world politics" mean? It is without a doubt a reference to the imperialist and colonial wars that are sure to reduce or eliminate the democratic progress of countries in conflict. We will return to this issue.

The surprising assertion that democracy is linked to the workers' and socialist movement has also been confirmed by the history of the following decades: the defeat of the socialist Left because of its divisions, its mistakes, and its weakness—in Italy, in Germany, in Austria, in Spain—leading to the triumph of fascism, with the backing of the principal forces of the bourgeoisie and the abolition of all forms of democracy during many long years (in Spain for decades).

The relationship between the workers' movement and democracy is eminently dialectical: democracy needs the social movement and vice versa—the proletarian struggle needs democracy in order to develop.

If democracy has become superfluous or annoying to the bourgeoisie, it is on the contrary necessary and indispensable to the working class. It is necessary to the working class because it creates the political forms (autonomous administration, electoral rights, and so on) which will serve the proletariat as fulcrums in its task of transforming bourgeois society. Democracy is indispensable to the working class because only through the exercise of its democratic rights, in the struggle for democracy, can the proletariat become aware of its class interests and its historic task.

Rosa Luxemburg's formulation is complex. In a first moment, she seems to say that it is thanks to democracy that the working class can struggle to transform society. Would this mean that in the non-democratic countries such a struggle is not possible? On the contrary, insists the Polish revolutionary, it is *in the struggle* for democracy that class-consciousness develops. She is thinking, no doubt, about a country like tsarist Russia—which included Poland—where democracy did not yet exist, and where revolutionary consciousness was awakening precisely in the fight for democracy. This is what one will see a few years later, during the Russian Revolution of 1905. But she may also be thinking, and probably is, about Wilhelmine Germany, where the fight for democracy was far from being won but found in the socialist movement its principal historic subject. In any case, far from neglecting the "democratic forms," which she distinguishes from their bourgeois exploitation and manipulation, she strictly associates their fate with that of the workers' movement.

What, then, are the important democratic forms? In 1898, she mentions three above all: universal suffrage, the democratic republic, and self-administration; later—for example on the subject of the Russian Revolution of 1918—she will add the democratic freedoms: freedom of expression, freedom of the press, and the right to organize. What about parliament? Luxemburg doesn't deny democratic representation as such, but she is wary of parliamentarism in its current form: she considers it "a specific instrument of the bourgeois class state, a way to make capitalist contradictions mature and develop."9 She will return to this debate a few years later in polemical articles against Jean Jaurès and the French socialists whom she accuses of wanting to arrive at socialism by way of "the peaceful swamp of senile parliamentarism." The degradation of this institution is revealed in its submission to the executive power: "[t]he idea, rational in itself, that the government shouldn't cease being the instrument of the majority of popular representation, is turned into its contrary by the practice of bourgeois parliamentarism: namely the servile dependence of popular representation on the survival of the present government." She gives credit, in this context, to the French revolutionary socialists who have understood that the legislative action of parliament—useful for extracting some laws favorable to the workers—cannot substitute for the organization of the proletariat for the conquest of political power by revolutionary means.[10]

One finds analogous arguments in an essay of 1904 titled "Social Democracy and Parliamentarism." With the mordant irony that makes her polemics so electrifying, she takes up the issue of "parliamentary cretinism," that is, the illusion according to which parliament is the central axis of social life and the motive force of world history. The reality is completely otherwise: the enormous forces of world history, in point of fact, act outside of the bourgeois legislative chambers. Far from being the absolute product of democratic Progress, parliamentarism is a historically determined form of the class rule of the bourgeoisie. At the same time, in a dialectical movement—Luxemburg cites Hegel—with the rise of the socialist movement, parliament must become "one of the most powerful and indispensable instruments of the class struggle" of the workers, serving as a tribune of the popular masses and a locus of agitation for the socialist revolution. But one cannot then effectively defend democracy, and the parliament itself, against reactionary maneuvers except by the *extra-parliamentary* action of the proletariat. The direct action of the proletarian masses "in the streets"—for example, in the form of a general strike—is the best defense in the face of threats against universal suffrage. In short, the challenge for socialists is to convince "the working masses to count more and more on their own forces and on their autonomous action and not to consider parliamentary struggles as the central axis of political life."[11] We will return to this.

The Contradictions of the Democratic Bourgeoisie: Militarism, Colonialism

The "really existing bourgeois democracies" are characterized by two profoundly antidemocratic dimensions that are closely linked: militarism and colonialism. In the first case, it is the question of an institution: the army, hierarchical, authoritarian, and reactionary, which constitutes a sort of absolutist state within the democratic state. In the second, it is a question of the imposition, by force of arms, of a dictatorship over the colonized peoples by the Western empires. As Luxemburg recalls in *Reform or Revolution?*, its class character always obliges the bourgeois state, even a democratic bourgeois state, to accentuate its coercive activity in the domains that serve the interests of the bourgeoisie, "namely militarism and customs and colonial policy."[12] The denunciation of this "coercive activity," militarist and imperialist, will be one of the principal axes of Luxemburg's critique of the bourgeois state.

From the capitalist point of view,

> [m]ilitarism has become indispensable. First, as a means of struggle for the defense of "national" interests in competition against other "national" groups. Second, as a means of investment of financial and industrial capital. Third, as an instrument of class domination over the laboring population inside the country. In themselves, these interests have nothing in common with the development of the capitalist mode of production.
>
> What demonstrates best the specific character of present-day militarism is the fact that it develops generally in all countries as an effect, so to speak, of its own internal, mechanical motive power, a phenomenon that was completely unknown several decades ago. We recognize this in the fatal character of the impending explosion, which is inevitable in spite of the complete indecisiveness of the objectives and motives of the conflict. From a motor of capitalist development militarism has changed into a capitalist malady.[13]

Luxemburg predicted, in 1898, a world war sparked by competition between national capitalist powers and the uncontrollable dynamics of militarism. This is one of those dazzling intuitions found throughout *Reform or Revolution?* even if she could not, of course, predict "the circumstances" of the conflict.

Militarism within and colonial expansion without are closely linked and lead to a decline, a degradation, a degeneration of bourgeois democracy:

As a result of the development of the world economy and the aggravation and generalization of competition on the world market, militarism and the policy of big navies have become, as instruments of world politics, a decisive factor in the interior as well as in the exterior life of the great states. If it is true that world politics and militarism represent a rising tendency in the present phase of capitalism, then bourgeois democracy must logically move in a descending line. In Germany the era of great armaments began in 1893, and the policy of world politics, inaugurated with the seizure of Tsingtao [Quingdao], were paid for immediately with the following sacrificial victim: the decomposition of liberalism, the shift of the Centre Party from opposition to government. The recent elections to the Reichstag of 1907, fought under the sign of German colonial policy, were, at the same time, the historical burial of German liberalism.[14]

In the course of the twentieth century, one will see other such sacrifices of democracy demanded by militarism—in Europe (Spain, Greece) as well as in Latin America—much more serious and dramatic than the examples cited here. Nevertheless, Luxemburg's analysis is broader: she describes the growing weight of the army in the political life of the bourgeois democracies, not only in imperialist competition but also as an internal factor within bourgeois societies counterposed to the rising workers' struggles. In an anti-militarist article of 1914, she shows two underlying tendencies that reinforce the political preponderance of military institutions in the bourgeois state:

These two tendencies are, on the one side, imperialism, which leads to a massive increase in the size of the army, the cult of savage military violence, and a dominating and arbitrary militarism with regard to legislation; on the other side, the workers' movement that is also undergoing a massive development, emphasizing class antagonisms, and bringing about military intervention more and more frequently by the army against the proletariat in struggle.[15]

This "savage military violence" is exercised within the framework of imperialist politics, above all against colonial peoples who are subjected to a brutal oppression that has nothing "democratic" about it. Bourgeois democracy produces in its colonial policy autocratic and dictatorial forms of domination. The question of colonialism is touched upon but not very developed in *Reform or Revolution?* But later, in a 1902 article about Martinique, Luxemburg will denounce the French colonial massacres in Madagascar, the American war of conquest in the Philippines, and England's in Africa, and finally the aggression against China committed by the French, English, Russians, Germans, Italians, and Americans working together.[16]

Luxemburg will return to the crimes of colonialism, in particular in *The Accumulation of Capital* (1913). Picking up the thread of her relentless critique of colonial politics, she turns to the chapter on primitive accumulation in volume 1 of *Capital*, however observing that it is not a question of an "initial" moment but of a permanent tendency of capital: "Here it is not a question of primitive accumulation, the process continues to our own time. Each colonial expansion is accompanied by an obstinate war against indigenous economic and social conditions, as well as the violent plundering of their means of production and their labor force." Accumulation leads to the permanent military occupation of the colonies and the brutal repression of their uprising, of which the classic examples are found in English colonialism in India and French colonialism in Algeria.[17] In fact, this permanent primitive accumulation continues today in the twenty-first century, with methods different—but no less ferocious—than those of classical colonialism.

Rosa Luxemburg also mentions in *The Accumulation of Capital* the case of what could be called internal colonialism in the largest modern bourgeois democracy, the United States: in the course of the conquest of the West, with the help of the railroads, the Native Americans were driven out or exterminated with firearms, with whiskey, and with syphilis and the survivors enclosed in "reservations" like savage beasts—another tragic example of the contradictions of bourgeois democracy.[18]

Democracy and the Conquest of Power:
The Hammer Blow of Revolution

Let's return to *Reform or Revolution?* now to examine the issue of the relationship between democracy and the conquest of power. Bernstein and his "revisionist" friends believed in the possibility of changing society through gradual reforms within the framework of bourgeois democratic institutions, notably parliament, where Social Democracy might one day become the majority. For reasons that we have already mentioned above, Rosa Luxemburg could only reject this strategy: "There was no doubt for Marx and Engels about the necessity of having the proletariat conquer political power. It is left to Bernstein to consider the chicken coop of bourgeois parliamentarism as the organ by means of which we are to realize the most formidable social transformation of history—the passage from capitalist society to socialism."[19] This revolutionary conquest of power will be democratic not because it will be realized within the framework of bourgeois democratic institutions, but because it will be the collective action of the great majority of the population: "This the difference between the Blanquist style coups d'état carried out 'by a militant minority,' initiated without concern for the moment and, in fact, always at the wrong time, and the conquest of political power by the great conscious mass of the people."[20]

Continuing her polemic, she derides Bernstein's reformist approach and puts forward a powerful argument to justify the need for revolutionary action.

> Fourier's scheme of changing, by means of a system of phalansteries, the water of all the seas into tasty lemonade was surely a fantastic idea. But Bernstein, proposing to change the sea of capitalist bitterness into a sea of socialist sweetness, by progressively pouring into it bottles of social reformist lemonade, presents an idea that is merely more insipid but no less fantastic.
>
> The production relations of capitalist society approach more and more the production relations of socialist society.

But, on the other hand, its political and juridical relations establish between capitalist society and socialist society a steadily rising wall. This wall is not overthrown, but is on the contrary strengthened and consolidated by the development of social reforms and the course of democracy. Only the hammer blow of revolution, that is, the conquest of political power by the proletariat, can break down this wall.[21]

The image of the "hammer blow" makes one think immediately of Marx's statement in his writings on the Paris Commune (1871) about the necessity, for proletarian revolution, of "smashing" the capitalist state apparatus. The idea is essentially identical, even if Luxemburg doesn't cite the writings of Marx. This "hammer blow" is even more indispensable if one considers the role of the growing militarism and of the army in the political system. What does this consist of concretely? By what means can this conquest of power be carried out? What revolutionary strategy or tactic does Luxemburg propose? This is a not a theme developed in *Reform or Revolution?* but here and there she suggests that the "classic" revolutionary methods—insurrection, barricades—are not excluded. Not only the revisionists but also the leadership of the German Social Democratic Party referred insistently to the preface written by Friedrich Engels in 1895 at the time of the new edition of Marx's work *The Class Struggles in France* (1850); in this text the old leader seems to consider that these methods of struggle have been rendered obsolete by progress in the military arts—canons and modern rifles—giving a strategic advantage to the army.

In fact, Engels's original wording was much less categorical, the published version being considerably "watered down" by the party leadership (of which Luxemburg was ignorant). Engels was outraged by this manipulation; in a letter to Karl Kautsky on April 1, 1895, he wrote, "To my amazement, I see today in *Vorwärts* an extract from my introduction, reproduced without my knowledge, and arranged in such a way that I appear to be a peaceful worshipper of legality at any price. Also, I would like the introduction to appear in *Neue Zeit*

without any cuts, so that this shameful impression is cleared up."
Friedrich Engels died a few months later; the complete text never
appeared in *Neue Zeit*, nor, of course, in the reedition of Marx's book.
It would have to wait for the Russian Revolution of 1917, after which
it was finally published in the 1920s.[22] Here is the response of Luxemburg to the "legalistic" argument:

> When Engels in the Preface to *The Class Struggles in France*
> revised the tactics of the modern workers' movement, oppos-
> ing to the barricades the legal struggle, he did not have in
> mind—as every line of that preface demonstrates—the prob-
> lem of the definitive conquest of political power, but rather
> that of the current everyday struggle. He doesn't analyze the
> attitude of the proletariat with regard to the capitalist state at
> the moment of the seizure of power, but its attitude within
> the framework of the capitalist state. In a word, Engels gives
> instructions to the *oppressed* proletariat, and not to the victo-
> rious proletariat.[23]

In fact, her interpretation is disputable. It is not a question, with
Engels, of the role of barricades in the "current everyday struggle"!
What is interesting in this passage is the attitude of the author of
Reform or Revolution? with regard to the question of "armed," "insur-
rectional," and "illegal" methods of struggle—traditional methods
from the revolutions of 1789 to 1871—which she refused to exclude
from the political arsenal of the proletariat. She was not wrong to do
so, since all of the great revolutionary fights of the twentieth century,
victorious or defeated—the two Russian revolutions (1905, 1917), the
Mexican Revolution (1910–19), the German Revolution (1918–19),
the Spanish Revolution (1936–37), and the Cuban Revolution (1959–
61), to cite only some examples—made use of these "illegal" and
"extra-parliamentary" methods.

But the revolutionary method that she favored, as we know, is
the mass strike, the "natural and spontaneous form of all great revolutionary action of the proletariat." In fact, this is a method that
abounds in a very great variety of initiatives of struggle: economic

and political strikes, demonstration or fighting strikes, mass strikes and partial strikes, fights at the barricades, "a sea of phenomena, eternally new and ceaselessly moving and changing." Of course the mass strike "does not replace or render superfluous direct and brutal confrontations in the street." The experience of Russia in 1905 shows that "combat at the barricades and the head-on confrontation with the forces of the state constitutes the highpoint in the contemporary revolution, a phase in the process of struggle of the proletarian mass."[24] The confrontation is not eliminated but located at the "climax" of the struggle, which obviously gives it an important role.

Luxemburg will return to Engels's preface in the watered-down version of the German Social Democratic Party, the only one known in her period—which definitely annoyed her—in her speech to the founding convention of the Communist Party of Germany (KPD—Spartakusbund) in December 1918. This time around it was not a question of pretending, as in 1898, that it referred to the "current everyday struggle": "With all the knowledge that specialists in the domain of military science have at their disposal, Engels demonstrates here . . . that it is completely vain to believe that working people can take their revolution to the streets and come out victorious." He was wrong, and this document served, she observes, to reduce the party's activity exclusively to the parliamentary realm. Without excluding the "revolutionary use of the National Assembly" as a tribune, she sees the seizure of power by workers' and soldiers' councils, as in Russia in October 1917, as the road to follow.[25]

Rosa Luxemburg gives no recipes; she is betting on the creativity of the revolutionary movement. She limits herself to this simple observation: "Democracy is indispensable, not because it makes the conquest of political power by the proletariat unnecessary, on the contrary, it makes it both necessary and possible to take power."[26] But this conquest of power comes by way of an institutional rupture, a radical subversion, capable of breaking the legal and political wall of the capitalist state; it comes by the "hammer of the revolution."

Socialist Democracy and Bourgeois Democracy (1918)

We are not going to discuss here the question of democracy in a socialist society, which goes beyond the scope of this essay. What interests us here is what Luxemburg writes in her little book on the Russian Revolution, on the subject of bourgeois democracy. It is important to emphasize that the manuscript of 1918 fraternally criticizing the Bolsheviks' errors in the area of democracy in no way suggests that Luxemburg subscribed to bourgeois democracy. It says explicitly that the historic task of the proletariat is "to create in place of bourgeois democracy, socialist democracy." Let's look at her argument in her polemic with Trotsky:

> "As Marxists," writes Trotsky, "we have never been idol worshippers of formal democracy." Surely, we have never been idol worshippers of socialism or Marxism either. Does it follow from this that we may throw socialism on the scrap-heap, á la Cunow, Lensch, and Parvus [a faction of the Social Democratic Party], if it becomes uncomfortable for us? Trotsky and Lenin are the living refutation of this answer.
>
> "We have never been idol worshippers of formal democracy." All that that really means is: We have always distinguished the social kernel from the political form of bourgeois democracy; we have always revealed the hard kernel of social inequality and lack of freedom hidden under the sweet shell of formal equality and freedom—not in order to reject the latter but to spur the working class into not being satisfied with the shell, but rather, by conquering political power, to create a socialist democracy to replace bourgeois democracy—not to eliminate democracy altogether.[27]

Rosa Luxemburg returns here to the "classic" distinction, already formulated in *Reform or Revolution?*, between the democratic form, equality, and formal freedom and the bourgeois content, inequality, and the killing of freedom. But this time she affirms the solution clearly: neither bourgeois democracy nor the dictatorship of a revolutionary elite, but a socialist democracy with a new social content.

Rosa Luxemburg had foreseen in 1914 "the intervention of the army in struggle against the proletariat." As we know, in January 1919, Rosa Luxemburg herself, Leo Jogiches, Karl Liebknecht, and other Spartacists would be assassinated, victims of this "military savage violence" that she had denounced and which had taken place within the framework of a respectable, constitutional (bourgeois) democracy. What Luxemburg had not foreseen, even in her worst nightmares, was that this political assassination by the counterrevolutionary military officers would take place under the aegis of a government led by the SPD, the German Social Democratic Party.

Translated by Dan La Botz

4. Revolution and Freedom

Rosa Luxemburg and the Russian Revolution

In January 1919, Rosa Luxemburg, founder of the German Communist Party (Spartacus League) was murdered by a unit of "Free Corps" (Freikorps), those counterrevolutionary military and officer bands—the future breeding ground of the Nazi party—that were brought to Berlin by the Social Democratic minister, Gustav Noske, to crush the Spartacist uprising.

She was therefore, like Emiliano Zapata in that same year, a "casualty of history." But her message remained alive in what Walter Benjamin called "the tradition of the oppressed"—a message that was at once, and inseparably, Marxist, revolutionary, and humanist. Whether in her critique of capitalism as an inhuman system; in her fight against militarism, colonialism, and imperialism; or in her vision of an emancipated society, her utopia of a world without exploitation, alienation and borders, this revolutionary humanism runs like a red thread through all of her political writings—but also through her correspondence, her moving prison letters, which have been read and read again by successive generations of young activists in the labor movement. Perhaps the most important aspect of her Marxist humanism are her reflections on the importance of freedom and democracy in the socialist revolutionary process.

Faced with the historical failure of the dominant currents of the workers' movement, that is to say, on the one hand the inglorious collapse of the so-called real socialism—the heir of sixty years of Stalinism—and on the other hand the passive submission (unless it is an active adhesion?) of Social Democracy to the—neoliberal—rules of the world capitalist game, the alternative represented by Rosa Luxemburg, that is to say a socialism that is both authentically revolutionary and radically democratic, appears more relevant than ever.

. . .

As a militant of the workers' movement in the tsarist empire—she had helped found the Social Democracy of Poland and Lithuania, affiliated to the Russian Social Democratic Labor Party—she had criticized the tendencies, in her opinion too authoritarian and centralist, of the theses defended by Lenin before 1905. Her criticism coincided, on this point, with that of the young Trotsky in *Our Political Tasks* (1904).

At the same time, as a leader of the left wing of German Social Democracy, she fought against the tendency of the trade union and political bureaucracy, or the parliamentary representations, to monopolize political decisions. The Russian mass strikes of 1905 seemed to her to be an example to be followed in Germany as well: she trusted more in the initiative of the working class base than in the wise decisions of the leading bodies of the German labor movement.

Learning about the events of October 1917, she wrote in prison, in the Summer 1918, a manuscript where she at the same time praised the Bolshevik revolutionary leadership and criticized some of their actions. Paul Levi, her lawyer (and lover), who was one of the Spartacist leaders, persuaded her not to publish these notes. The document appeared, under the title *The Russian Revolution*, only after her death, in 1922, by initiative of the same Paul Levi, after his expulsion from the German Communist Party in 1921. Did she change her mind on some issues after the November 1918 Revolution in Germany, as some of her Communist friends (Clara Zetkin, Adolf Warszawski) argued? The question remains open for historians to decide. In any case, *The Russian Revolution*—in spite of some shortcomings we will discuss below—is one of the most important documents of revolutionary thinking in the twentieth century.

Her well-known biographer J. P. Nettl has a rather derogatory view of the pamphlet: "Her general conclusions had little or nothing to do with the details she was criticizing; rather she was applying well-established, systematic conclusions to a new set of facts. 'The Russian Revolution' happened to the title of the particular frame passing through Rosa Luxemburg epidiascope at the time."[1]

This seems to me a very strange assessment. The value of Luxemburg's piece is precisely the dialectical unity between revolutionary principles and a precise analysis of detailed facts. And for her, obviously, the Russian Revolution was not some "frame passing through her epidiascope" (an optical device for projecting images), but a decisive issue of life and death for the international labor movement!

The first thing that must be said about this writing is that Rosa Luxemburg saluted the Russian Revolution of October 1917 as a great emancipatory historical act. The first section of her pamphlet is a warm homage to the Bolshevik revolutionary leadership. As her biographer Paul Frölich observes, "[S]he never paid to any people or party such an enthusiastic homage as the one she did to the Bolsheviks in this writing."[2]

Luxemburg had nothing but contempt for the social democratic German or Russian critics of the October Revolution. In her view, the developments in Russia during 1917 are a decisive refutation of the doctrinaire theory that Kautsky shared with the Mencheviks, according to which Russia, as an economically backward and predominantly agrarian land, was supposed not to be ripe for a proletarian revolution. These people, who regarded only a bourgeois revolution as feasible in Russia, denounced the radical wing of the Russian labor movement, the Bolsheviks, for attempting to go beyond these limits, toward socialism.

Rejecting these anti-revolutionary arguments, she openly and unhesitatingly sides with the Russian "radical wing," the only one that took the initiative to call for "all power to the soviets." For her, there is not any doubt that

the Bolshevik tendency performs the historic service of having proclaimed from the very beginning, and having followed with iron consistency, those tactics which alone could

save democracy and drive the revolution ahead. All power
exclusively in the hands of the worker and peasant masses, in
the hands of the soviets—this was indeed the only way out of
the difficulty into which the revolution had gotten; this was
the sword stroke with which they cut the Gordian knot, freed
the revolution from a narrow blind-alley and opened up for it
an untrammeled path into the free and open fields.[3]

In her eyes, all the "moderate wings" of the Russian labor movement failed by their refusal to take a revolutionary stand. The Bolsheviks were the only ones who had the courage to do so: "The party of
Lenin was thus the only one in Russia which grasped the true interest of the revolution in that first period. It was the element that drove
the revolution forward, and, thus it was the only party which really
carried on a socialist policy."

Moreover, she saw the October Revolution not as a Bolsehvik
"putsch" or a sort of "coup d'état," as so many critics pretended, but
as the result of a truly consistent revolutionary political orientation,
which enjoyed the support of the popular classes:

> It is this which makes clear, too, why it was that the Bolshe-
> viks, though they were at the beginning of the revolution a
> persecuted, slandered and hunted minority attacked on all
> sides, arrived within the shortest time to the head of the revo-
> lution and were able to bring under their banner all the genu-
> ine masses of the people: the urban proletariat, the army, the
> peasants, as well as the revolutionary elements of democracy,
> the left wing of the Socialist-Revolutionaries.

Unlike Leon Trotsky's theory of permanent revolution, to which her
strategic views on the Russian revolution are similar, she does not
ground them in an analysis of the uneven and combined development of the Russian mode of production, but on a broad historical
vision of the revolutionary movements in the past:

> [T]he Russian Revolution has but confirmed the basic lesson
> of every great revolution, the law of its being, which decrees:

either the revolution must advance at a rapid, stormy, resolute tempo, break down all barriers with an iron hand and place its goals ever farther ahead, or it is quite soon thrown backward behind its feeble point of departure and suppressed by counter-revolution. To stand still, to mark time on one spot, to be contented with the first goal it happens to reach, is never possible in revolution.

Once more, she denounces the reformist Social Democratic views, whose "parliamentary cretinism" (Marx) makes them utterly unable to understand the dynamics of a real revolutionary process: "He who tries to apply the home-made wisdom derived from parliamentary battles between frogs and mice to the field of revolutionary tactics only shows thereby that the very psychology and laws of existence of revolution are alien to him and that all historical experience is to him a book sealed with seven seals."[4]

The conclusion of this first section is a powerful testimony to her profound admiration for the Bolshevik leadership:

> Whatever a party could offer of courage, revolutionary far-sightedness and consistency in an historic hour, Lenin, Trotsky and all the other comrades have given in good measure. All the revolutionary honor and capacity which western Social-Democracy lacked was represented by the Bolsheviks. Their October uprising was not only the actual salvation of the Russian Revolution; it was also the salvation of the honor of international socialism.

Some anti-Bolshevik interpretations of her pamphlet tend to skip this first section. This is an outright falsification. The starting point of her reflections was an outspoken and strongly argued support for the October revolutionaries, whose *consistency* she opposed to the inconsistent and dishonorable policies of German and Western Social Democracy. As so often in her writings, her comments here are at the same time a political and a *moral* judgment: ethics and strategy were for her inseparable moments of the revolutionary action.

This being said, Luxemburg's solidarity with the Bolsheviks did not exclude *criticism*, and in fact *most of the pamphlet was composed of critical arguments*. They do not contradict the first section, but they are its necessary complement: unconditional but critical support is the general spirit of this unique document. It should be said that these critical comments do not concern details but issues that she considered decisive for the future of the Russian Revolution.

The first two criticisms, dealing with the land and the nationality issues, are the least persuasive. She believed that the Bolsheviks made a fatal mistake by distributing the land to the peasants, thus creating a great obstacle for a future socialization of agriculture. As Paul Frölich soberly observes, "[I]f the Bolsheviks tried to oppose themselves to the sharing of the land . . . they would need to make a war against the peasants. That would be the end of the revolution."[5] The same applies to the issue of the right of nations to self-determination, which she rejected in the name of internationalism. Her criticism of the Bolshevik principle—in fact, not always implemented in practice—of letting the people of the various nations that composed the tsarist empire decide of their future (separation or union) is quite contradictory to her ardent plea for democracy in the revolutionary process.

The democratic argument is by far the most important contribution of the pamphlet to revolutionary socialist theory. It constitutes a consistent and forceful critique of some key aspects of the Bolshevik policy, so to say "from inside" the revolutionary camp. But it is much more than just a negative critical comment: it presents a positive view of why freedom and democracy are not "luxuries" but *indispensable dimensions of any process of socialist transformation of society*. This belief was, in one way or another, present in all her previous political writings, but in this pamphlet it is for the first time presented in a systematic, explicit, and concrete way.

Her first comments concerned the Constituent Assembly, forcibly dissolved by the Bolsheviks after they seized power. The Bolsheviks argued that since the Constituent Assembly had been elected well before the decisive turning point, the October Revolution, and its composition reflected a past scenario and not the new state of affairs, it had to be dissolved. Luxemburg agreed but immediately added: If this is the case, why not call for new elections to a new Constituent Assembly, reflecting the new situation after October? Trotsky's argument that "the cumbersome mechanism of democratic institutions" is not adapted to revolutionary periods seems to her particularly objectionable, since it seems to refuse "any popular representation whatsoever which might come from universal popular elections during the revolution."

Did she change her opinion on this issue because she supported, in Germany, after the November Revolution of 1918, the call for "all power to the councils"? According to her Communist friends (Clara Zetkin et al.), this is indeed the case and it is for this reason that Luxemburg did not want to publish her pamphlet.

Whatever the conclusion on this specific issue, it should be emphasized that the discussion on the Constituent Assembly is not, by far, her main argument. Her concern goes much deeper and has to do with the most essential aspects of a socialist revolutionary process: Can it take place without freedom and without democratic institutions? For her, the obvious answer is no, and this leads her to a sharp critique of the Bolshevik policy:

> To be sure, every democratic institution has its limits and shortcomings, things which it doubtless shares with all other human institutions. But the remedy which Trotsky and Lenin have found, the elimination of democracy as such, is worse than the disease it is supposed to cure; for it stops up the very living source from which alone can come correction of all the innate shortcomings of social institutions. That source is the active, untrammeled, energetic political life of the broadest masses of the people.

Luxemburg had always been an unmerciful critic of bourgeois democracy and its formal institutions, but she is not willing to give up the socialist principle of democracy:

We have always distinguished the social kernel from the political form of bourgeois democracy; we have always revealed the hard kernel of social inequality and lack of freedom hidden under the sweet shell of formal equality and freedom—not in order to reject the latter but to spur the working class into not being satisfied with the shell, but rather, by conquering political power, to create a socialist democracy to replace bourgeois democracy—not to eliminate democracy altogether.

The issue, in fact, is much broader than the question of the institutions: it has to do with *freedom*. According to Luxemburg "it is a well-known and indisputable fact that without a free and untrammeled press, without the unlimited right of association and assemblage, the rule of the broad masses of the people is entirely unthinkable." And she adds a phrase that has been often quoted, and to some extent is a quintessential argument for the indissoluble unity between *freedom* and *revolution:*

Freedom only for the supporters of the government, only for the members of one party—however numerous they may be—is no freedom at all. Freedom is always and exclusively freedom for the one who thinks differently. Not because of any fanatical concept of "justice" but because all that is instructive, wholesome and purifying in political freedom depends on this essential characteristic, and its effectiveness vanishes when "freedom" becomes a special privilege.

This outstanding apology of freedom has not much to do with bourgeois liberalism. She has no respect for bourgeois property rights, the established legal order, or traditional parliamentarism. For Luxemburg, freedom and democracy are not at all contradictory with the *dictatorship of the proletariat*, the famous Marxian formulation for the transitional period beginning with the socialist revolution. According to her, once the proletariat seizes power,

it should and must at once undertake socialist measures in the most energetic, unyielding and unhesitant fashion, in other words, exercise a dictatorship, but a dictatorship of the class, not of a party or of a clique—dictatorship of the class, that means in the broadest possible form on the basis of the most active, unlimited participation of the mass of the people, of unlimited democracy.

She therefore opposes her conception of "class dictatorship," as a collective form of power, which includes all the indispensable democratic freedoms, to the one being implemented by the Bolsheviks, which in her view has more in common with Jacobinism than with socialism (a viewpoint, by the way, already voiced by the young Leon Trotsky in his polemic with Bolshevism in 1904):

> Without general elections, without unrestricted freedom of press and assembly, without a free struggle of opinion, life dies out in every public institution, becomes a mere semblance of life, in which only the bureaucracy remains as the active element. Public life gradually falls asleep, a few dozen party leaders of inexhaustible energy and boundless experience direct and rule. Among them, in reality only a dozen outstanding heads do the leading and an elite of the working class is invited from time to time to meetings where they are to applaud the speeches of the leaders, and to approve proposed resolutions unanimously—at bottom, then, a clique affair—a dictatorship, to be sure, not the dictatorship of the proletariat but only the dictatorship of a handful of politicians, that is a dictatorship in the bourgeois sense, in the sense of the rule of the Jacobins.

"Only the bureaucracy remains the active element"—it is difficult not to recognize the prophetic dimension of this warning. By their drastic restriction or suppression of democratic rights and freedoms, the Bolshevik leaders involuntarily helped to create the golem that was to destroy them. Despite Lenin and Trotsky's belated efforts, bureaucracy soon—after 1924—became hegemonic, and, under the leadership of Joseph Dzhugashvili Stalin, swiftly proceeded to marginalize and expel the Bolshevik leaders of the October Revolution, before exterminating them, together with thousands of other faithful Communists, in the monstrous purges of the late 1930s. This was no more a Jacobin dictatorship but a Thermidorian, or better, a Bonapartist one, in a modern version, based on police terror, mass murder, and an extended network of concentration camps. Rosa Luxemburg could not predict this, but she saw the danger: once freedom and democracy are suppressed, bureaucracy becomes the dominant force.

One can find a similar prediction in an anarchist document from the same period, a letter by Errico Malatesta to his friend Luigi Fabbri from July 1919. The Italian anarchist does not deny that the Bolsheviks are authentic revolutionaries, but he believes their politics will lead to fateful consequences for themselves and for the revolutionary process:

> Lenin, Trotsky and their comrades are assuredly sincere revolutionaries . . . and they will not be turning traitors—but they are preparing the governmental structures which those who will come after them will utilize to exploit the Revolution and do it to death. They will be the first victims of their methods and I am afraid that the Revolution will go under with them. History repeats itself: mutatis mutandis, it was Robespierre's dictatorship that brought Robespierre to the guillotine and paved the way for Napoleon.[6]

It is important to emphasize that Luxemburg did not ignore the extremely difficult and precarious situation of the revolutionary power in 1918, and the impossibility for the Bolsheviks to implement an ideal socialist democracy. She simply calls on them not to present their policies as a model for the Communist movement:

> It would be demanding something superhuman from Lenin and his comrades if we should expect of them that under such circumstances they should conjure forth the finest democracy, the most exemplary dictatorship of the proletariat and a flourishing socialist economy. By their determined revolutionary

stand, their exemplary strength in action, and their unbreakable loyalty to international socialism, they have contributed whatever could possibly be contributed under such devilishly hard conditions. The danger begins only when they make a virtue of necessity and want to freeze into a complete theoretical system all the tactics forced upon them by these fatal circumstances, and want to recommend them to the international proletariat as a model of socialist tactics.

In the conclusion of the pamphlet, Luxemburg once more shows her solidarity with the Bolsheviks. In the last analysis, whatever the disageements, they represent the hope for a revolutionary future:

> What is in order is to distinguish the essential from the non-essential, the kernel from the accidental excrescencies in the politics of the Bolsheviks. In the present period, when we face decisive final struggles in all the world, the most important problem of socialism was and is the burning question of our time. It is not a matter of this or that secondary question of tactics, but of the capacity for action of the proletariat, the strength to act, the will to power of socialism as such. In this, Lenin and Trotsky and their friends were the first, those who went ahead as an example to the proletariat of the world; they are still the only ones up to now who can cry with Hutten: "I have dared!"

This does not mean, of course, that her criticisms on the issue of democracy and freedom are not important: they are decisive! But they cannot be separated from her enthusiastic support for the Russian revolutionaries. She hoped that their difficulties would be resolved by a revolution in Germany: as we know, this did not happen, thanks to Friedrich Ebert, Phillip Scheidemann, Gustav Noske, and their ilk.

The importance of Luxemburg's reflections on the dialectical link between socialist revolution and democratic freedoms is so great because they open an horizon that goes well beyond the historical discussion on the rights and wrongs of Lenin and Trotsky during the first years of the Russian Revolution. Any attempt to rebuild a revolutionary movement, a revolutionary socialist perspective, in the twenty-first century cannot ignore her arguments. They are a precious and enduring legacy for future generations.

5. Western Imperialism against Primitive Communism

A New Reading of Rosa Luxemburg's Economic Writings

The discussion on Rosa Luxemburg's theories of imperialism has mainly focused on the economic argument—the schemes of reproduction, the process of circulation, the need for "external" markets, etc. There is, however, another dimension at least as important: the struggle of imperialism against precapitalist economies, the ruthless destruction of "natural" and peasant economies, many of them being forms of *primitive communism*. Luxemburg's interest in primitive communist societies is documented by her *Introduction to Political Economy*, and the imperialist war against them is discussed both in this work and in the last chapters of *The Accumulation of Capital*. A wholly original approach to the evolution of social formations, running counter to linear "progressive" views of bourgeois ideology, is outlined in these reflections. Present Indigenous struggles, for example in Latin America against multinational oil or mining companies, illustrate the topicality of Rosa Luxemburg's argument in the twenty-first century.

A rarely discussed aspect of Luxemburg's economic writings is her passionate interest in precapitalist communities. Let us start with her *Introduction to Political Economy (Einführung in die Nationalökonomie)*, a work published by Paul Levi in 1925.[1] The manuscript was

drafted in prison in 1914–15, based on notes from her course in political economy at the school of the German Social Democratic Party
(1907–14). The text is doubtless unfinished, but it is astonishing all
the same that the chapters devoted to primitive communist society
and its dissolution take up more space than those devoted to market
production and the capitalist economy together. This unusual way of
approaching political economy is probably why this work has been
neglected by most of the Marxist economists (Ernest Mandel, the
author of the preface to the French edition, is an exception) and even
by the biographers of Rosa Luxemburg (except for Paul Frölich). As
for the Marx-Engels-Lenin-Stalin Institute of East Berlin, responsible
for the reedition of the text in 1951, it claims in its preface that the
book is a "popular presentation of the fundamental features of the
capitalist mode of production," forgetting that almost half the book
is devoted to precapitalist formations. In fact, the central theme of
the book is the analysis of social formation that she calls *primitive
communist societies*—and their opposition to capitalist market society.[2] A wholly original approach to the evolution of social formations,
running counter to linear and evolutionist "progressive" views, is
outlined in this text.

What lies behind Luxemburg's interest in so-called primitive
communes? On the one hand, it is obvious that she seeks to use
the very existence of such ancient communist societies as a tool to
shake up and even destroy "the old notion of the eternal nature of
private property and its existence from the beginning of the world
[Die alte Vorstellung von der Ewigkeit des Privateigentums und
seinem bestehen von Anbeginn der Welt]." It is because bourgeois
economists cannot even conceive of communal property and cannot
comprehend anything that does not resemble capitalist civilization
that they stubbornly refuse to recognize the historical phenomenon
of communities. On the other hand, Luxemburg sees primitive communism as a precious historical reference point for criticizing capitalism, for unveiling its irrational, reified, anarchic character, and
for bringing to light the radical opposition between use value and
exchange value.[3] Luxemburg's aim, then, is to find and "save" every-

thing in the primitive past that may prefigure modern socialism, at least up to a point.

Like Marx and Engels, Luxemburg looked closely at the writings of the historian Georg Ludwig von Maurer on the ancient Germanic commune (*Mark*); like them, she marveled at the democratic and egalitarian functioning of this communist formation and at its *social transparency*:

> One cannot imagine anything simpler and more harmonious [*Harmonischeres*] than the economic system of the ancient German communes [*alten germanische Mark*]. The whole mechanism of social life is there in plain view. A rigorous plan and a robust organization frame the activity of each member and integrate him as an element of the whole. The immediate needs of daily life and their equal satisfaction for all: such is the point of departure and the destination of this organization. All work together for all and decide together about everything.
>
> From where does this all flow and on what is based this organization and the power of the whole over the singular? It is nothing other than communism of the soil and earth; in other words, the common property of the main means of production by the workers.[4]

Luxemburg highlights the features of this communitarian formation that *oppose it to capitalism* and make it in certain respects humanly superior to modern bourgeois civilization: "More than two thousand years ago . . . then, among the Germanic peoples there reigned a state of affairs fundamentally different from the current situation. No state with written and constraining laws, no split between rich and poor, between masters and workers."[5]

Relying on the work of the Russian historian Maxime Kovalevsky, in whom Marx had been quite interested earlier on, Luxemburg stresses the *universality* of the agrarian commune as a general form of human society at a certain stage of its development, a stage one finds among American Indians, the Incas, and the Aztecs as well as among the Kabyls, African tribes, and the Hindus. The Peruvian example seems most significant, and here too she cannot refrain from suggesting a comparison between the Inca *marca* and "civilized" society: "The modern art of being exclusively nourished by the work of others and making leisure the attribute of power was foreign to this social organization in which common property and the general obligation to work constituted deeply rooted popular customs." She thus manifests her admiration for "the incredible resistance of the Indian people and of the agrarian communist institutions of which, despite the conditions, vestiges have been preserved right into the nineteenth century."[6] Some twenty years later, the eminent Peruvian Marxist thinker José Carlos Mariátegui advanced a thesis that presented striking convergences with Luxemburg's ideas, though he was very probably unacquainted with her remarks on Peru: to win over the peasant masses, modern socialism has to look to the Indigenous traditions that go back to Incan communism.

The most important author in this area was, for Luxemburg as for Marx and Engels, the American anthropologist Lewis Morgan. Starting from his classic work *Ancient Society* (1877), she went further than Marx and Engels, developing an entire grandiose vision of history, a heterodox conception of the age-old evolution of humanity, in which contemporary civilization "with its private property, its class domination, its masculine domination, its constraining State and marriage" appears as a mere parenthesis, a transition between primitive communist society and the communist society of the future. The revolutionary idea of the link between past and future lies at the heart of this visionary perspective:

> The noble tradition [*adelige* Überlieferung] of the remote past thus held out a hand to the revolutionary aspirations of the future, the circle of knowledge closed harmoniously, and, in this perspective, the present world of class domination and exploitation, which claimed to be the ne plus ultra of civilization [*Kultur*], the supreme goal of universal history, was no longer anything but a miniscule and transitory

stage on the great civilizational forward march [*Kulturvor-marsch*] of humanity.[7]

From this standpoint, the European colonization of Third World peoples struck Luxemburg as a fundamentally inhuman and socially destructive enterprise. The English occupation of India was a revealing case in point: it ravaged and shattered the traditional communist agrarian structures, with tragic consequences for the peasantry. Rosa Luxemburg shared Marx's conviction that imperialism brings economic progress to colonized nations, even if it does so "by the ignoble methods of a class society (*niederträchtigen Methoden einer Klassengesellschaft*).[8] Still, while Marx, without concealing his indignation at such methods, emphasized the *economically progressive* role of the railways introduced by England into India, Luxemburg placed greater stress on the *socially harmful* consequences of capitalist "progress":

> The old ties were broken; the peaceful isolation of communism from the world was shattered and replaced by quarrels, discord, inequality, and exploitation [*Hader, Zwietracht, Ungleichheit und Ausbeutung*]. This produced huge *latifundia* [*latifundien*] on the one hand, and an enormous mass of millions of farmers without means [*mitelloser bäuerlicher Pächter*] on the other. Private property celebrated its entrance into India, and with it typhus, hunger, and scurvy, which became permanent guests on the Ganges plains.[9]

This difference from Marx probably corresponds to a distinct historical stage that allowed a new way of looking at colonized countries, but it is also the expression of Luxemburg's particular sensitivity to the social and human qualities of primitive communities.

This argument is developed not only in the *Introduction to Political Economy* but also in *The Accumulation of Capital*, where Luxemburg again criticizes the historical role of English colonialism and expresses outrage at the criminal scorn that the European conquerors displayed toward the old system of irrigation. Capital, in its blind unbridled greed, "is incapable of seeing far enough to recognize the value of the economic monuments of an older civilization"; colonial politics provoked the decline of this traditional system, and as a result, starting in 1867, famine began to claim millions of victims in India. As for French colonization in Algeria, she saw it as characterized by a systematic and deliberate attempt at destruction and dislocation of communal property, leading to the economic ruin of the Indigenous population.[10]

In chapter 27 of *The Accumulation of Capital,* "The Struggle against Natural Economy," she shows that all European colonialist enterprises share a similar brutal policy of uprooting precapitalist Indigenous social structures :

> Since the primitive associations of the natives are the strongest protection for their social organizations and for their material bases of existence, capital must begin by planning the systematic destruction and annihilation of all the non-capitalist social units that obstruct its development. . . . Each new colonial expansion is accompanied, as a matter of course, by a relentless battle of capital against the social and economic ties of the natives, who are also forcibly robbed of their means of production and labor power.[11]

Marx had already denounced, in the chapter on "Primitive Accumulation" from *Capital,* the violence of colonial policies. The new argument suggested by Rosa Luxemburg is that "primitive accumulation" is a *permanent trait of imperialist expansion,* from the sixteenth century till now:

> The accumulation of capital, seen as an historical process, employs force as a permanent weapon, not only at its genesis but down to the present day. . . . The method of violence, then, is the immediate consequence of the clash between capitalism and the organizations of a natural economy that would restrict accumulation. . . . British policy in India and French policy in Algeria are the classical examples of the application of these methods by capitalism.[12]

While the main concept used by Luxemburg in this chapter, and in most of the book, to define these Indigenous precapitalist structures is "natural economy," she also refers, occasionally, to *communism*, as when describing "the ancient economic organizations of the Indians—the communist village community" that "had been preserved in their various forms over thousands of years, in spite of all the political disturbances during their long history" but were finally disrupted by British colonialism. Or, when discussing the French colonial policy in Northern Africa, which "persevered for fifty years in its systematic and deliberate efforts to destroy and disrupt communal property" but finally miscarried "because of the difficulties in substituting at one stroke bourgeois private property for the ancient clan communism."[13]

Most of the examples discuss European colonialism, but she draws a parallel with US expansionist policies and their cruel war against Indigenous communities:

> In 1825, the Congress of the Union under Monroe decided to transplant the red Indians from the East to the West of the Mississippi. The redskins put up a desperate resistance; but all who survived the slaughter of forty red Indian campaigns were swept away like so much rubbish and driven like cattle to the West to be corralled in reservations like so many sheep.[14]

Above and beyond any specific examples, Luxemburg denounced the entire colonial system—whether Spanish, Portuguese, Dutch, English, American, or German, in Africa, Asia, and the Americas. She adopted the viewpoint of the victims of capitalist modernization. As she emphasizes in the *Introduction to Political Economy*, "For primitive peoples, in the colonial countries where primitive communism once reigned, modern capitalism constitutes a sudden catastrophe, an unspeakable misfortune [*unsägliches Unglück*] replete with the most frightful suffering."[15]

According to her, the struggle of the Indigenous populations against the imperial metropolis admirably manifests the tenacious resistance of the old communist traditions against the avid quest for profits brutally imposed by capitalist "Europeanization." The bourgeoisie instinctively grasped a dark connection between this resistance of ancient communism and "the new Evangelism of the proletarian masses" in Europe. Thus, the French National Assembly insisted, in 1873—just a few years after the massacre of the Paris Commune—that ancient forms of communal property in Algeria must be annihilated because they "favor the development of communist tendencies in the spirits."[16] Reading between the lines, one can discern here the idea of an alliance between the anticolonial struggle of the colonized peoples and the anticapitalist struggle of the modern proletariat as a revolutionary convergence between the old and the new communism.

Does this mean, as Gilbert Badia—the author of a remarkable biography of Rosa Luxemburg, and one of the rare scholars who has examined this aspect of her work critically—believes, that she presents the ancient structures of colonized societies in an excessively rigid "black-and-white contrast with capitalism"? According to Badia, Luxemburg contrasts the old communities, "endowed with every virtue and conceived as virtually immobile," with the "destructive function of a capitalism that no longer has any progressive aspects whatsoever. We are far removed from the conquering bourgeoisie evoked by Marx in the *Manifesto*.[17]

These objections strike us as unjustified, for the following reasons:

- Rosa Luxemburg did not conceive of the old communities as immobile or frozen; on the contrary, she shows their contradictions and transformations. She stresses that "through its own internal evolution, primitive communist society leads to inequality and despotism.[18]
- She does not deny the economically progressive role of capitalism, but she denounces the "ignoble" and socially regressive aspects of capitalist colonization.
- While she highlights the most positive aspects of primitive communism, in contrast with bourgeois civilization, she does

not fail to point out its flaws and limitations: locally restricted outlooks, a low level of labor productivity and of development toward civilization, helplessness in the face of nature, brutal violence, a permanent state of war between communities, and so on.[19]

- In fact, Luxemburg's approach is very different from the one Marx adopted in his 1848 hymn to the bourgeoisie; in contrast, it is very close to the spirit of chapter 31 of *Capital* ("Genesis of the Industrial Capitalist"), where Marx describes the "barbarities" and "atrocities" of European colonization.

Furthermore, on the topic of the Russian rural commune, Luxemburg's view is much more critical than Marx's. Taking Engels's analysis of the late-nineteenth-century decline of the *obschtchina* as her starting point, she highlights the historical limits of traditional communities in general, and the need to surpass them.[20] Then, looking toward the future, she parts company from the Russian populists, insisting on "the fundamental difference between the worldwide socialist economy (*sozialistischen Weltwirtschaft*) of the future and the primitive communist groups of prehistory."[21]

Be that as it may, Luxemburg's writings on this theme are much more than an erudite glance at economic history: they suggest *another way* of conceiving of the past and the present, of social historicity, progress, and modernity. By confronting capitalist industrial civilization with humanity's communitarian past, Rosa Luxemburg breaks with linear evolutionism, positivist "progressivism," and all the banally "modernizing" interpretations of Marxism that prevailed in her day.

Are the Indigenous communities in Chiapas, Mexico, in the Andean mountains of Peru, Bolivia, and Ecuador, or in the Amazonian forests of Peru and Brazil remnants of "primitive communism"? In any case, it is in the name of their communal traditions, and their forms of collective social and economic organization, in harmony with their natural environment, that they—as well as their sisters on other continents—fight against the destructive endeavors, in the name of "growth," "modernization," or "progress," of local or multinational agro-business enterprises, oil companies, and big cattle ranchers. The resistance of peasant and Indigenous communities against brutal and violent forms of *permanent primitive accumulation* continues in our days . . .

6. Rosa Luxemburg and Internationalism

Few figures in the socialist movement have been as committed to the categorical imperative of internationalism as Rosa Luxemburg. She was Jewish, Polish, and German, yet her true "fatherland" (or "motherland") was the Socialist International. This universalism and cosmopolitanism perhaps explains why she never showed a particular interest in Judaism or the plight of European Jewry. Like Heinrich Heine, Karl Marx, and Leon Trotsky, she belonged to the tradition described by Isaac Deutscher as "the non-Jewish Jew": brilliant intellectuals who transcended what they saw as the too-narrow boundaries of Judaism, but who nevertheless contained "something of the essence of Jewish life and intellect." As revolutionaries, they lived and thought beyond national boundaries and dreamed of internationalism: "As Jews they were natural pioneers of this idea: Who was better qualified to preach an international Socialism founded on equality than Jews freed from all orthodoxy and nationalism—Jews or non-Jews?"[1]

It goes without saying that internationalism was not the monopoly of Jewish Marxists! The majority of its proponents in the workers' movement came from other backgrounds, but undoubtedly, many Jews can be found among the most notable figures in the turn-of-the-century international revolutionary movement. This was particularly true in Eastern Europe, so-called Yiddishland. The best known of these are only the tip of the proverbial iceberg: Lev D. Trotsky (Bronstein), Julius Martov (Tsederbaum), Raphael Abramovich, Lev Deutsch, Pavel Axelrod, Mark Liber (Goldman), Fyodor Dan

(Gurvitch), Lev Kamenev (Rosenfeld), Karl Radek (Sobelsohn), Gregory Zinoviev (Radomilsky), Jacob Sverdlov, David Riazanov (Goldendach), Adolf Warszawski, Isaac Deutscher, etc. That does not include specifically Jewish socialist organizations such as the Bund or leftist Zionists, or intellectual Jews who originated in Eastern Europe but participated in the German workers' movement: Leo Jogiches, Parvus (Israel Helphand), Arkadi Maslow (Isaac Tchereminski), August Kleine (Samuel Heifiz), and many others.

Rosa Luxemburg clearly belonged to this constellation of revolutionary internationalist non-Jewish Jews. Born in 1871 to an assimilated family of Jews in Zamość, Poland, she did not receive a proper Jewish education: her parents—Eliasz Luxemburg and Lina Löwenstein—descended from a line of rabbis and Talmudists, were cultured middle-class folk more interested in Polish and German literature than in Yiddish culture.

Luxemburg's obstinate internationalism precluded any particular interest in the destiny of Jewish communities. As she wrote in a well-known passage from a letter to her friend Mathilde Wurm in February 1917,

> What's the point of going on about the particular suffering of the Jewish people? For me, the unfortunate victims of rubber plantations in Putumayo, Europeans' shuffling back and forth of black African bodies like they were playing ball, touch me just as much. You remember the account of Von Trotha's campaign in the Kalahari in the works of the High Command?: "And the groans of the agonized, the cries of those driven mad by thirst echoed in the sublime silence of eternity." That "sublime silence of eternity," into which so many cries *disappear,* explode in my chest so forcefully that I simply cannot keep a special place in my heart for the ghetto. I feel at home anywhere in this vast world where there are clouds, birds, and tears.[2]

This perspective also explains her critique of the Jewish Bund, whose "separatism" she rejected, although this did not prevent her from recognizing its contribution in an April 1903 article: according to Luxemburg, the Jewish Bund was uniquely positioned to reach the masses of Yiddish-language workers in Russia and Poland, and to win them over to socialism.[3] Luxemburg was even more critical of Zionism, considering it as more of a "social-patriotic" deviation; she thus paid it little notice since for the Jewish masses in Eastern Europe, it was at that time less influential than the Bund.

Of course, distancing herself from any commitment to Jewish causes did not prevent virulent antisemitic campaigns against her, in Poland in particular. As Andrzej Niemojewski, a nationalist Polish intellectual, wrote in 1910, "As all Jews hate non-Jews, Rosa Luxemburg's Social Democrats have a passionate hatred for Poland." The "social-patriotic" (in Luxemburg's view) PPS (Polish Socialist Party) presented similar views in its publication, maintaining that Luxemburg's party, the SDKPiL (the Social Democracy of the Kingdom of Poland and Lithuania), served "Jewish" rather than proletarian interests. In a series of biting articles in her party's mouthpiece, *Mtot* (The Hammer), she counterattacked the slander: Antisemitism in Poland has become "the common flag sheltering political arrogance and cultural barbarity," inspired by the brutish madness of the Russian Black Hundred.[4]

Similar attacks occurred in Germany: antisemitic caricatures of "Rosa the Bloody" appeared in the bourgeois press, and, along with other Social Democratic Jews, she was accused of taking part in the conspiracy of the "Great Sanhedrin." Less evident but more painful for Luxemburg were the attacks from German Social Democrats from the right wing of the party, such as Gustav Noske and Wolfgang Heine, who accused Polish and Russian Jews of abusing German hospitality. In his memoirs, published in 1947, Noske defended himself against accusations of antisemitism but insisted that "Jewish Marxists from Eastern Europe" had played a negative role in the SPD.[5]

It is interesting to note that Rosa Luxemburg strongly supported Jean Jaurès during the campaign in defense of Captain Dreyfus, despite opposing the socialist leader Millerand's entrance into a bourgeois government. She also clearly recognized the role of antisemitism in this confrontation: "In the Dreyfus case, four social factors have arisen that concern class struggle: militarism, chauvinism-nationalism, antisemitism, and clericalism." She adds that these are "direct enemies of the socialist proletariat."[6]

That said, in reading her writings, it is clear that she underestimated the force and the danger of antisemitism. Very few comments in her writings deal with antisemitism in Germany, which as we know was to change the course of European history in the following decades. To be clear, she was not the only socialist at the time to make that error in judgment. Nevertheless, unlike Lenin, Trotsky, or even Kautsky, she never attempted to analyze the pogroms in tsarist Russia . . .

These oversights have to do with her general attitude toward the national question, which was the problematic and questionable reverse of her radical internationalism. The most well-known example was of course her attitude toward the national claims in Poland, her native country. Not only did she oppose the call for Polish national independence—the flag of "social-patriots" of Pilsudski's party, the PPS—but she even rejected Bolshevik support for the right of Polish self-determination, including the right to its separation from the Russian Empire.[7] Until 1914, she based her position on economic arguments: the Polish economy was already integrated into the Russian economy and therefore Polish independence was a purely utopian demand, held only by the aristocracy or layers of the petite bourgeoisie—a surprising underestimation of the nationalist sentiment shared by the great majority of the Polish people. Furthermore, she conceived nations as an essentially "cultural" phenomenon and therefore proposed "cultural autonomy" as a solution for the national demands. What is missing in this approach, however, is precisely the political approach to the national question put forward in Lenin's writings: the democratic right to self-determination.[8]

Nevertheless, at least in the introduction to the 1905 collection *The Polish Question and the Socialist Movement*, she broached this problem in a much more open and dialectical manner. In this writing, she makes a precise distinction between the legitimate rights of each nation to independence—which "follow from elementary principles of socialism"—and the desirability of this independence specifically for Poland, which she rejects. She also insists that national oppression is "the most barbaric and intolerable form of oppression," which can only give rise to "hostility and rebellion."[9] However, several years later, in her notes on the Russian Revolution (1918)—which contain perfectly legitimate criticism of the authoritarian and antidemocratic measures taken by the Bolsheviks—she once again rejects any reference to a nation's right to self-determination as "empty petit-bourgeois phraseology."[10]

Most of the discussion surrounding Rosa Luxemburg's radical internationalism, including by the author of this writing, is particularly and even uniquely interested in the very questionable dim view she takes of the political rights of nation-states. What is missing in this approach, however, is the positive side of her perspective, her rich contribution to the Marxist conception of proletarian internationalism, and her obstinate refusal to yield to a nationalist and chauvinistic siren's call. In the following pages, let us briefly summarize this contribution.

Beyond Eurocentrism

Georg Lukács, in his chapter "The Marxism of Rosa Luxemburg" in *History and Class Consciousness* (1923), proclaims that the dialectical category of "totality" is "the bearer of the principle of revolution in science."[11] He considered the writings of Rosa Luxemburg in general and *The Accumulation of Capital* in particular a striking example of this dialectical approach.

One could say the same of her internationalism: she analyzes, discusses, and judges all social and political questions from the perspective of totality, i.e., from the perspective of the interests of the international working class. This dialectical totality was for her no abstraction, empty universalism, or conglomeration of undifferentiated beings: she was perfectly aware that the international proletariat is a human plurality consisting of peoples with their own cultures, languages, and histories whose living and working conditions could vary significantly.

For Luxemburg, the universal proletariat was not limited to Europe and the United States. For example, in *The Accumulation of Capital*, she goes to great lengths in discussing the working class of South Africa: citing an English author, James Bryce (1877), she observes

> the most vivid description of the methods used in South Africa to solve the "labor problem." Here we learn that Black people are forced to work in the mines and plantations of Kimberley, Witwatersrand, Natal, and Matabeleland by stripping them of all land and cattle. . . . Finally, they are simply press-ganged into the wage system of capital by means of violence, imprisonment, and the whip.[12]

One can find in her writings one of the first attempts in turn-of-the-century socialism to go beyond Eurocentrism. Very early on, well before most of her comrades, she was an active opponent of the colonial politics of European imperialist powers and made no effort to hide her empathy for the struggles of colonized peoples.

This anticolonialist choice is one of the reasons that Luxemburg refused, from her arrival in Germany and the ranks of German Social Democracy, all concessions to militarism, military spending, and naval expeditions. While the right wing of the SPD—Wolfgang Heine and Max Schippel—was ready to negotiate agreements with the kaiser's administration on these questions, Luxemburg openly denounced their capitulations, which they supposedly justified in the name of "creating jobs."

Peter Nettl, author of an important biography of Luxemburg— very well documented but limited by its more academic than socialist approach, is deceived in describing Luxemburg's internationalist opposition to such concessions as "a dry and formal exercise" based on the belief that unemployment is a necessary stimulant for the class struggle![13]

Luxemburg's anticolonialist position shows up very early: in 1902, in a short article entitled "Martinique," she denounces crimes of Western colonialism in the Antilles and in Madagascar, where the French colonial government gunned down thousands to force this "free people to submit to the yoke"—but also in the Philippines, and especially in China, where France, England, Russia, and Germany "united in a great League of Nations" to massacre and pillage the country. Nor does she overlook North American imperialism, recalling how "Washington's sugar-cane senate [*Zuckerkartell-Senat*]" sent "cannon after cannon, battleship after battleship, and millions upon millions of dollars in gold to Cuba to sow death and destruction."[14]

The Opium War against China was in her eyes a striking example of what passed for the "civilization" and "culture" that the European powers claimed to bring to "Barbarian" peoples:

> The period in which China was opened up to European civilization—i.e., to the exchange of commodities with European capital—was inaugurated by the Opium Wars, in which China was forced to buy opium from Indian plantations in order to make money for British capitalists . . . Thus began the glorious "opening up" of China to European civilization in the shape of the opium pipe.

Thanks to the superiority of their weapons, the imperialist forces imposed "the freedom of commerce" on China, profiting from it to pillage the country; the opening of Chinese ports was "paid for with streams of blood, carnage, and destruction."[15]

Naturally, German imperialism was one of the principal objects of her polemics. Take for example the bloody German colonial wars in South West Africa (1904). In a speech from June 1911, she explains,

> The Hereros are a black people who have lived for centuries on their own territories. . . . Their "crime" is that they have not yielded to the white slavers . . . and have defended their homeland [*Heimat*] against the foreign invaders. . . . In this war, German weapons are once again covered in "glory." . . . Men were gunned down and women and children . . . were forced into the scorching desert.[16]

Luxemburg also denounces German colonial ambitions—in competition with French colonialism—that gave rise to incidents in Morocco in 1911. Criticizing Eduard Bernstein's propositions in favor of an "equality of the rights of trading nations" to Morocco, she insists that the only legitimate right of the country is that of the Indigenous peoples of Morocco to rebel against colonial enterprises.[17]

If the internationalist Rosa Luxemburg is this sympathetic to the resistance of colonized peoples, it is because one of the essential characteristics of the process of colonialization is the deliberate destruction of traditional collectivist forms of ownership of Indigenous peoples—primitive communism—in favor of private property. These forms were of the greatest interest to Luxemburg: in her courses at the SPD School before the war, published posthumously in 1925 by Paul Levi, she discusses in depth diverse forms of primitive communism around the world, which emphasize the fallaciousness of "the old idea of the eternal character of private property and its existence from the beginning of the world."[18]

Rosa Luxemburg was convinced that "agrarian communism [is] an international primitive form of development that appeared among all races and in all parts of the world." Drawing inspiration from the work of Morgan, Marx and Engels declared that primitive communism was the universal ancient past of human history: in their writings, Luxemburg observes—in a concise summary of the whole dialectical view of history—that "the noble human survivals of the dim past offered a hand to the revolutionary efforts of the future."[19]

Luxemburg was particularly interested in Latin America and Andean civilizations, recalling that Marx's friend Maxime Kovalevsky had concluded that "Peru's legendary Inca Empire embraced the same primitive agrarian communism that Maurer pointed out had existed among the ancient Teutons." She uses the term "Inca communism" to describe this social formation: to be sure, the Inca Empire was despotic and parasitic, but this "harsh system of exploitation nevertheless left intact the interior life of communities and their democratic communist institutions." She does not hide her admiration for "the incredible resistance of the indigenous people and of agrarian communist institutions, whose vestiges, despite the circumstances, had managed to survive into the nineteenth century."[20]

What was, for Luxemburg, the destiny of this "democratic communism" in the imperialist era? Imperialist expansion led above all to the brutal destruction of these precapitalist forms, with dramatic consequences for the Indigenous populations. Above all, this destructive dynamic obeys economic forces since these forms are an obstacle to the penetration of capitalism. According to Luxemburg, this was the case with the British colonization of India:

> The old ties were broken; the peaceful isolation of communism from the world was shattered and replaced by quarrels, discord, inequality, and exploitation. This produced huge *latifundia* on the one hand, and an enormous mass of millions of farmers without means on the other. Private property celebrated its entrance into India, and with it typhus, hunger, and scurvy, which became permanent guests on the Ganges plains. [21]

In certain cases, however, the extermination of communal traditions also had clear political motivations. Luxemburg here cites the French colonization of Algeria: the victors of the Commune had a law passed in 1873 that aimed for the total destruction of the primitive commune of the Arabs, considered as "a form that preserves communist tendencies." For Luxemburg, the French bourgeoisie had understood the affinity "between the old communist traditions that, in colonized countries, offered a tenacious resistance to the pursuit of profit," and the new proletarian Gospel that emerged with the Paris Commune of 1871.[22]

Whether in India or North Africa, European colonialism collided with the determined resistance of "ancient social bonds and communist institutions that protected the individual from the activities of European capitalist exploitation and the politics of European finance"[23]—a resistance that translated into the struggle of Indigenous populations against colonial forces.

In her most important writing on economics, *The Accumulation of Capital* (1913), Luxemburg puts forth a hypothesis that will prove to be very relevant in the following decades: capitalist accumulation on a global scale, founded on violence, is not only an early stage of the system but a permanent process of coercive expropriation.

In colonized countries, "capital takes as its first task the systematic destruction and annihilation of non-capitalist social structures that obstruct its expansion. This is not simply a question of primitive accumulation because this process continues to the present day." Violence, she adds,

> has been a permanent mechanism of the historic process of accumulation since its inception. But primitive societies, for which this is a life or death struggle, have no other recourse but resistance and a fight to the finish—exhaustion or obliteration. Continual military colonial occupation ensues along with indigenous revolts and the colonial expeditions designed to suppress them, the permanent phenomena of colonial regimes. The use of force is the direct consequence of the clash of capitalism with the structures of natural economy that oppose limits to its accumulation.[24]

Very few socialists from this era denounced colonial expeditions, and even fewer went so far as to legitimize the resistance and struggles of colonized peoples. This attitude reveals the authentically universal nature of Luxemburg's internationalism, although Europe was undeniably the central focus of her attention.

Rosa Luxemburg clearly distanced herself from the linear and Eurocentric conception of history as "the progress of civilization," whose benefits would be doled out by the most advanced nations to those closer to barbarism—a discourse that had long served to legitimize colonialism.

The idea of an alliance between the communist traditions of colonized peoples and the communist program of the modern workers' movement is only hinted at in the writings of Rosa Luxemburg. It would, however, find an explicit strategic formulation of these ideas in the writings of a Peruvian Marxist from the 1920s, José Carlos Mariátegui. Mariátegui did not know of Luxemburg's writings on economics (he did not read German . . .), but he did use the term "Inca communism" to describe the rural communes that formed the basis of the ancient Andean Empire. In his opinion, which was denounced as "romantic" and "populist" (in the Russian sense) by (Stalinist) Soviet Marxists and their Peruvian disciples, Peru's Indigenous collectivist traditions were still alive and well in the twentieth century and could serve as a point of departure for a convergence with the modern proletarian communist movement.[25]

Against War: Either/Or!

Rosa Luxemburg readily perceived the growing danger of war in Europe and tirelessly denounced Imperial Germany's war preparations. In September 1913 she gave a lecture in Bockenheim, close to Frankfurt, that concluded with a solemn internationalist sermon: "If they think we're going to raise instruments of murder against our French or other brothers, we will cry—Never!"[26] The public prosecutor immediately accused her of "calling for civil disobedience against the law." A trial took place in February 1914 in which Luxemburg testified without compromise to denounce militarism and the politics of war, citing a resolution from the Brussels Congress of 1868 of the First International: in case of war, workers should call for a general strike. Her speech was printed by the socialist press and became a sort of little classic of antiwar literature. She was sentenced to one year in prison, but it was only after the start of the war in 1915 that imperial authorities dared to arrest her.[27]

One might perceive Luxemburg's conviction that the workers would oppose imperial warmongering as an illusion, but, curiously, we can find a similar position by an author one does not normally suspect of having Marxist/revolutionary sympathies—Max Weber! In a text drafted before the war, "The Economic Foundations of 'Imperialism,'" he explains the "pacifist sympathies . . . of the proletarian masses" by saying that "coercive imperialist politics that succeed from without" reinforce "from within" the opponents of the proletariat, the class system, and the dominant parties. Many capitalists are pro-war, but, even among the privileged strata, there are those who fear "a violent upheaval of power in favor of the have-nots amid the chaos following a defeat."[28] Which is precisely what almost took place in Germany between November 1918 and January 1919 . . .

As we know, Rosa Luxemburg was part of the stubborn minority who, back in August 1914, had refused to join the choir of supporters of the "national defense" at the heart of the workers' movement. She immediately tried to organize opposition to the war, which she saw as an inter-imperial conflict. On the evening of August 4, following a vote by the deputies of the SPD for war appropriations, she gathered in her apartment to contemplate the resistance movement with some friends: Franz Mehring, Julian Marchlewski, Ernst Meyer, Hermann and Käthe Dunker, and Wilhelm Pieck. They were subsequently joined by Clara Zetkin and Karl Liebknecht. A few months later, they began publishing the opposition review *The International*.

Luxemburg's writings during these decisive months never yielded to the official bellicose ideology; rather, she developed ever more critical arguments against what she saw as the dramatic betrayal by the leaders of the SPD of the principles of proletarian internationalism. In the spring of 1915, she published an article in *The International*—"Perspectives and Projects"—and directed her sarcasm at Kautsky's position, arguing that "[t]he International is a weapon for times of peace, but not for times of war." She added that "[t]he historic call of the Communist Manifesto has received an important amendment and now proclaims, with Kautsky's correction: 'Workers of the world unite in times of peace, and in times of war, slit your throats.'" The capitulation of August 4 was thus in Luxemburg's eyes an unmitigated disaster: "This is a historic catastrophe of universal scope that dangerously complicates and hinders the liberation of humanity from capitalist domination."[29]

In attempting to explain what he calls her "growing hatred" for the dominant views of the SPD, her biographer J. P. Nettl points to a "powerful personal aspect": "the eternal and barely contained impatience and frustration of immigrants such as Rosa Luxemburg when faced with the cumbersomeness of German 'officials.'" I fear that this "personal" explanation is not very useful. As Nettl is obliged to admit, opposition to the war was not limited to foreign "immigrants" but rather included a number of homegrown Germans, such as Karl Liebknecht, Franz Mehring, and Clara Zetkin.[30] In fact, the reason for Rosa Luxemburg's indignation against the "social-patriotic" capitulation of August 1914 was not "immigrant impatience" but rather a lifelong struggle for internationalism.

Repeatedly imprisoned for her anti-militarist and anti-nationalist activities, Luxemburg drafted a famous pamphlet in prison in 1915, *The Junius Pamphlet: The Crisis of Social Democracy*, whose French editors (Julien Chuzeville and Eric Sevault) saw it as the "Communist Manifesto of the Imperial Age."[31] *Junius* defined world war as a sort of boomerang, where colonial violence would come back to Europe to strike the peoples of the Old World: "[T]he current world war marks a turning point in the course of imperialism. For the first time, the ferocious beasts that capitalist Europe has unleashed on other continents have in one single leap stormed into the heart of Europe." In her view, the most sinister aspect of the war was the fact that the "soldiers of socialism, the workers of England, France, Germany, Russia, Belgium . . . have been massacring each other for months at the behest of capital."[32]

It is in the *Junius Pamphlet* that the famous motto "socialism or barbarism" appears for the first time. Before the war, Rosa Luxemburg believed in the inevitability of the economic collapse (*Zusammenbruch*) of capitalism and thus in the necessary victory of socialism. The collapse of the Socialist International in August 1914 drove her to a new approach that established a real turning point in modern socialist thinking: socialism is not "inevitable"; it is one possibility among many, and no economic or historical law could guarantee its success. The other possibility was a sort of backsliding toward barbarism, but a modern barbarism of which world war was but a striking example. Although attributing it to Friedrich Engels, Luxemburg is nevertheless responsible for this innovative perspective:

> We now find ourselves faced with the same choice that Friedrich Engels confronted in the generation before ours, now

some forty years ago: either the triumph of imperialism and the decline of civilization, just as it occurred in ancient Rome, with depopulation, desolation, degeneration, and a vast grave-yard, or else the victory of socialism, that is, the conscious struggle of the international proletariat against imperialism and war, its modus operandi. That is the historical dilemma the world finds itself in, an "either/or" [*ein Entweder-oder*] that will tip the scales in one way or the other depending on the decision of a conscious proletariat.[33]

The end of the pamphlet is a cry of internationalist hope/despair. It is no longer a question of trying to prevent the future but a con-ditional judgment, a desperate gamble on the awakening of class consciousness: "This infernal and bloody nightmare will never cease until the workers . . . awaken from their stupor and offer each other a brotherly hand, until they drown out the chorus of the imperialist warmongers and howls of capitalist hyenas with the ancient and pow-erful proletarian war cry: Workers of the world, unite!"[34]

A few months later, she drafts another pamphlet, *Either/Or* (*Ent-weder-oder*) (1916), this time directed less at supporters of the war as at the indecision and half measures of the Social Democratic opposition led by Georg Ledebour, Hugo Haase, and their friends. Published underground by the Spartacists, the text highlights a verse from the Book of Revelation: "I wish that you were cold or hot, but because you are neither cold nor hot but just lukewarm, I will spit you out of my mouth."[35] . . . It is an interesting but little-known document: rarely mentioned by her biographers, it has never been translated into French. J. P. Nettl does not mention it but refers to Luxemburg's published articles on behalf of the Spartacus League as characterized by an "either/or frenzy," which judges everything "under the most extreme dichotomy."[36]

Indeed, faced with the horrors of world war, Rosa Luxemburg would tolerate no half-heartedness. In her eyes, a minority within the SPD—self-described as the "Working Group" (*Arbeitsgemeinschaft*) and led by Georg Ledebour, Hugo Haase, and others—was cruelly lacking in results, energy, and bite (*Schärfe*). In fact, after having voted in favor of war appropriations four times, they finally opposed them on December 21, 1915. But their justification sparked a revolt by Luxemburg: their opposition came not from a position of internationalism but because, due to Germany's military victories, "our borders are secure." That would then mean that if the military situation changed, they would once again side with the kaiser's government in its war strategies. What's more, taking this argument to its logical conclusion, the support of French, Belgian, Russian, and Serbian socialists for their own governments would also be legitimate since the German military was encamped on their territories; thus, their borders would not in fact be "secure."

Against what she considered a deplorable lack of consistency, Luxemburg proclaimed, "Either/or! Either the open and shameless betrayal of the International, as Heine, David, and Scheidemann are engaged in, or the serious and sacred respect for the International, to make it a fortress, a bastion of the worldwide socialist proletariat and of worldwide peace. For middle ground [*Mittelwege*] attitudes, hesitations, and half measures [*Halbheiten*], there can be no place."[37]

Luxemburg's obstinate rigidity was coupled with her unwavering conviction on the necessity of internationalism, which for her took the form of a genuine profession of faith: "The worldwide brotherhood of workers is for me the highest, most sacred thing in the world; it is my guiding star, my ideal, my homeland. I would rather lose my life than betray this ideal!"[38]

Toward a New International

As an addendum to the *Junius* and *Entweder-Oder* pamphlets, Luxemburg wrote a brief set of arguments entitled "Guiding Principles for the Tasks of International Social Democracy," which were approved by her comrades in the Spartacus League. It was essentially a call for a new Socialist International.

The document argues that "war has fractured the Second International. Its failure was revealed during the war in its incapacity to become a bulwark against national divisions." Given the betrayal of internationalist principles by the official socialist party leaders of the warring countries, Luxemburg and her comrades put out a call for a new workers' International.

In response to Karl Kautsky's argument that the Socialist International was viable only in times of peace, Rosa Luxemburg insisted that "[t]here can be no socialism outside of the international solidarity of the proletariat, just as there can be no socialism without class struggle. The socialist proletariat cannot renounce either the class struggle or international solidarity, whether in times of war or peace, without committing suicide." In an ironic challenge to the order to "defend the homeland" so common among the kaiser's ministers as well as Social Democrats surrounding Phillip Scheidemann, she proclaimed, "The homeland of the proletariat, whose defense takes precedence over all others, is the Socialist International."[39]

Luxemburg was convinced that as long as the capitalists were in power, militarism, imperialism, and war could never be avoided. In her opinion, international socialism was the only way to preserve world peace—not by bourgeois diplomatic propositions for "disarmament," "maritime freedom," "European political unions," "Central European customs unions," "national buffer states," etc.[40]

To prevent the new International from suffering the same fate as the Second, Luxemburg proposed relatively centralized operations predicated on international discipline:

- The center of gravity of the organization of the working class resides in the International, which in times of war . . . will make all tactical decisions.
- The duty to carry out the decisions of the International supersedes all other organizational duties. National sections that violate its decisions are automatically expelled from the International.[41]

In a personal letter to Luxemburg, her friend and comrade Karl Liebknecht criticizes this conception of the new International as "too mechanical and centralist" with "too much 'discipline' and not enough 'spontaneity,'" seeing the masses "too much as tools to carry out what the International wants and decides on and not enough on what they want and decide for themselves."[42] In a curious irony of history, these are almost word for word the very criticisms that Rosa Luxemburg had addressed to Lenin in a controversial article entitled "Organizational Questions of Russian Social Democracy" (1904).

Clearly, with these extreme measures, Luxemburg is trying to counter any demonstration of "social-patriotic" tendencies in the socialist movement. She emphasized that the most urgent task of the new International would be to "liberate the proletariat intellectually from the tutelage of the bourgeoisie, a tutelage made manifest in the influence of nationalist ideology."[43] Her understanding of "nationalism" is obviously not national culture or the national identity of different populations, but rather an ideology that proclaims the superiority of one nation over others, or that gives "the Nation" supreme moral and political worth, to which everything else must be subordinated ("Deutschland *über* Alles").

What is clear is that Rosa Luxemburg was prophetic in raising the alarm on the dangers of nationalism. The worst crimes of the twentieth century—Auschwitz, Hiroshima—were committed in the name of nationalism, national supremacy, national "living space" (Lebensraum), or the "defense of national interests." Stalinism itself was the product of the nationalist degeneration of the Soviet Union, which had become the defender of "socialism in one country."

One can criticize Rosa Luxemburg for having refused to recognize the right of national self-determination. However, she was all the more cognizant of the rights of colonized peoples to resist imperialist domination! Although she was not able to foresee genocide, Luxemburg was keenly aware of the dangers of national state policies: imperialist wars, colonialism, massacres, oppression of minorities, etc.

Rosa Luxemburg's Internationalism Today

Today's world is vastly different from the one that Rosa Luxemburg inhabited. Certainly, capitalism, militarism, imperialist wars, and lethal forms of nationalism are still with us—even if, since the beginning of the twentieth century, their forms have changed—and the need for an international coordination of the subaltern classes is still very relevant. What is missing nowadays, however, is organization on the scale of the first three Internationals. It is significant that the Fourth International, founded by Leon Trotsky and his comrades in 1938, still exists and is able to propose a number of interesting analyses, but it is not more than a small militant network with limited influence. As for the anti-globalization movement, which has admittedly succeeded in mobilizing significant grassroots movements based on an anti-systemic program, it has never grown into a force capable of unified action on an international scale.

Internationalism is now more necessary than ever, for a reason that did not exist in Rosa Luxemburg's time: the climate crisis. This is an unprecedented threat that puts the conditions for human life on earth in peril and is a direct result of the dynamics of expansion and destruction wrought by global capitalism. This crisis knows no borders and can only be contained by coordinated international action; this has been understood by millions of young people participating in worldwide school strikes responding to the call of an unlikely successor to Rosa Luxemburg—a sixteen-year-old militant Swedish environmental activist named Greta Thunberg.

To paraphrase a well-known quote from Walter Benjamin's *Theses on the Philosophy of History*, which Rosa Luxemburg would have approved of: either we pull the revolutionary "emergency brake" on the runaway train of industrial capitalist civilization, or it will continue speeding toward total ecological disaster. Now the time for half measures is past. It's either/or. *Entweder-oder . . .*

Translated by Lynne Sunderman

7. Georges Haupt, Internationalist

Under the Star of Rosa Luxemburg

I met Georges Haupt around 1969 through my doctoral advisor, Lucien Goldmann, another Romanian Jew. I was struck by his internationalist sensibility, as a researcher, teacher, and friend. Warm and charismatic, with much humor and a slightly ironic detachment, he won people's admiration and affection; we soon became friends. With his cultivated and cosmopolitan spirit, he spoke countless languages, but each with a slight Hungarian accent. He was no doubt the most Hungarian of all Romanian Jews-turned-naturalized French citizens . . . As much as he loved to tell stories about the leaders of international socialism, he was extremely reticent to share his own journey: his internment at Auschwitz—as evidenced by the number tattooed on his arm—his adherence to the Communist movement, his career as an academic and researcher in Romania, his break with Ceaușescu's Stalinist regime, and his departure for France (in 1958). It was only in bits and pieces that I could gradually pick up this moving life story. His sudden death in 1978 was a great shock for me as well as many of his friends and students in the "Haupt International." In April 1978 I published a brief homage in the weekly *Rouge*, of which I include a few excerpts:

> With the death of Georges Haupt we lose not only a scientific researcher of exceptional quality, but a man whose spiritual homeland was the international workers' movement. Born in Transylvania, a region that saw the ferocious clash

of Romanian and Hungarian nationalism, and a victim of
Nazi antisemitism that saw him interned at the age of twelve
in a concentration camp, early on he saw in socialist internationalism an alternative to nationalism and a way out of
the shattering of nations. Believing that the Romanian People's Republic and the USSR were a step toward realizing that
ideal, he initially joined the Romanian Communist Party, but
he soon perceived the bureaucratic and totalitarian character
of those so-called socialist regimes. Unlike so many others
who, once in the West, sought to vilify what they had previ-
ously loved, Georges Haupt remained faithful to the hope of
his youth. International socialism remained his clear-headed
passion, the humane and moral motivation for his work as a
researcher, a view of the world that was deeply anchored in
his personality and his work.[1]

We were in fact in love with the same woman, but without
jealousy: each simply believed he knew her better than the other.
That woman is, of course, Rosa Luxemburg. In his collection Bibliothèque Socialiste, under Maspero, I published my first book, *The
Theory of Revolution in the Young Marx* (1970), which was also my
doctoral dissertation under Goldmann's guidance. The book had
an obvious "Luxemburgist" slant, which is probably what attracted
Haupt's attention.

As a specialist on the history of the Second International, Haupt
was interested in different figures from that time, beginning with
the International's secretary, Camille Huysmans. But of all of the
personalities of international socialism, the one who most appealed
to him, the one he felt closest to, who sparked in him a "passionate attraction," as Fourier would say, was undoubtedly the Jewish
Polish revolutionary. At the beginning of 1969, along with "Johann
Knief"—a pseudonym of Boris Frankel, he organized an issue of the
journal *Partisans* entitled "The Living Rosa Luxemburg." Curiously,
it was dated "December–January 1969," although surely it was referring to December 1968. The spirit of 1968 haunts this fine publica-

tion, which contains a passionate text from Haupt on unedited letters from Luxemburg concerning disagreements with Lenin, Huysmans, and others. Ever optimistic, Haupt affirmed that "[n]owadays, we may speak of a true 'rediscovery' of Rosa and of 'Luxemburgism.' We need only mention the theoretical work of the SDS in Germany." I believe it was Frankel, whom I had known since my first stay in Paris in the early 1960s, who had invited me to write in the journal. But Haupt also read my paper: he found that the beginning was excellent but that the rest of the paper left something to be desired . . .

I only moved to Paris at the beginning of 1969, but with the sudden passing of Lucien Goldmann in 1970, I felt a bit "orphaned," and Georges Haupt took me under his wing. From 1970, I started regularly attending his seminar at Section VI of the École pratique des hautes études (the future École pratique des hautes études en sciences sociales), a marvelous place, a kind of little "International" where students from diverse countries and continents—with a large proportion coming from the Balkans—met for passionate discussions on the national question and the history of the workers' movement. As recounted by Claudie Weill in her fine text on this unique scientific and pedagogical experience, beginning in 1973, the seminar entitled "The Geography of Socialism" focused not only on Greece and the Balkans but on Europe and Latin America as a whole, with a particular emphasis on comparing the socialisms of Central Europe (Germany, Austria-Hungary) and Latin Europe (France, Italy).[2] The classroom was a small library at 105 Boulevard Saint-Michel, always crowded with students, some of whom had to sit on the floor. Oftentimes Haupt would invite witnesses of socialist history or foreign specialists to come and speak with us. I remember once hearing Alfred Rosmer recount his discussions on revolutionary tactics and strategies with "Vladimir Ilyich." When he was traveling, Haupt would occasionally ask me to fill in for him with his students. It was during one of these sessions that I was introduced to someone who, ten years later, would become my life companion: Eleni Varikas, who under Haupt's tutelage was preparing her master's thesis on the origins of the Greek labor movement.

Around 1972, Haupt proposed that we prepare an anthology on Marxists and the national question. Naturally, I was thrilled to accept. We decided that he would write a historical introduction, "The History of the Problem"; Claudie Weill would write the notes on each text; and I would write a more theoretical conclusion, "The Problem of History." A study of our respective texts reveals not only differences in our methods—Haupt's historical approach was much more subtle and complex—but also in our political interpretations: for my part, despite my admiration for Rosa, on the national question I stayed close to Lenin's positions, while Haupt's analysis avoided pronouncing judgment and aimed to grasp the logic of the differing positions.[3]

Several years later, in 1977, Haupt published in the journal *Pluriels* and essay entitled "Ideological Dynamism and Conservatism: Rosa Luxemburg at the Edge of Marxist Research in the National Domain," which was included in the subsequent posthumous collection *L'Historien et le mouvement social.*[4] Developing ideas that he had sketched out in the 1974 anthology, with a great deal of finesse, he analyzed the evolution of this Polish revolutionary's ideas in historical context, starting with her fundamental worldview: an uncompromising internationalism. For Haupt, Rosa Luxemburg played a major role in opening the debate on the national question in the international socialist movement. Rejecting the Russophobic conservatism of ideologues from the Second International, who swallowed whole Marx and Engels's positions on tactics—for the independence of Poland on the one hand, and for Turkey against the Russian Empire on the other—Rosa Luxemburg criticized Polish nationalism and defended the struggle for freedom by peoples oppressed by the Ottoman Empire. If one considers certain of her arguments, for example that the development of capitalism "condemns the separatist aspirations of Poland, AlsaceLoraine, and Bohemia to powerlessness" as both too economist and as disproven by history (a judgment that Haupt held his tongue on), one must nevertheless acknowledge the justice of her support for the struggle of the Armenians against the Ottoman state. Above all, as Haupt so clearly demonstrates, the stands she took were inspired by a steadfast internationalism and a rejection of nationalism and social patriotism in the workers' movement, an attitude that enabled her to resist the nationalist tidal wave that would submerge the whole of Europe in 1914.

In the conclusion of his essay, Haupt distances himself from the political culture of the Second International: imperialism awakened new historical forces, national liberation movements of "peoples without history," i.e., non-Western peoples who were ignored by a socialist movement that remained Eurocentric. Although Rosa Luxemburg contributed greatly to galvanizing socialist research and the school of thought on the national question, one might well ask whether she had not also "remained fixed on objectives called for by the historical moment," by the specific political and ideological context of the time. We must bear in mind, however, in *The Accumulation of Capital* her impressive lucidity in denouncing the crimes of Western imperialism.

From 1975–77, Georges Haupt published two volumes of Rosa Luxemburg's correspondence (Editions François Maspero)—*Vive la lutte!* and *J'étais, je suis, je serai*—with substantial introductions that significantly revitalized the approach both to her biography and to her thought processes. These texts are more personal than the essays on the national question and give more direct testimony of his attachment to the Jewish Polish revolutionary.

As Haupt writes in his brilliant presentation to *Vive la lutte!*, the letters of Rosa Luxemburg covering 1891–1914 are from a privileged source, rich in political enlightenment and often displaying high literary merit. They demonstrate the wide range of her interests and the extent of her theoretical, political, and human concerns. Her rich personality, sensibility, and culture find expression in these epistolary exchanges, in which passion and vehemence are mixed with a biting irony, and where bitterness and disappointment alternate with exuberant joy and limitless optimism. As Haupt writes, these are documents that project a "new, inner light" on the history of socialism.

Haupt often makes reference to J. P. Nettl's biography of Luxemburg, which he had published in his Bibliothèque Socialiste. But now and again he takes issue with what he sees as a work that is sometimes too academic, for example, as when Nettl claims that Luxemburg's "noisy" entrance into the debate on revisionism was inspired by a desire to "pursue a career" in German Social Democracy. Haupt soberly comments that this is due to a "false premise." Nettl makes assumptions that are foreign to the mindset of Rosa Luxemburg and her comrades, for whom the fight against revisionism was a bounden duty, a mission to accomplish, not a tactic aimed at furthering a "career." In fact, her combativeness embarrassed, shocked, and irritated the leading spheres of the party, not to mention her triple handicap of being a woman, a foreigner—and Jewish/Polish at that—and an intransigent Marxist. Nevertheless, her writings and activity as a teacher at the school of the SPD afforded her considerable influence; even a leader as moderate as August Bebel was moved to write, in a letter to Victor Adler in 1910, "Despite all the difficulties, I wouldn't want to be deprived of having this person in the party. At the party school, the radicals, revisionists, and syndicalists all praise her equally because she is the best teacher."[5]

The correspondence over these years reveals the diversity of Rosa Luxemburg's connections with the principal leaders of international socialism, from Camille Huysmans to Henriette Roland Holst, by way of G. Plekhanov and Jules Guesde. Always with a winning mix of empathy and distance, Haupt analyzes her ambivalent relationships with Karl Kautsky and Vladimir I. Lenin. Despite an initial skepticism, she ended up not only a political ally but a personal friend of Karl and Luise Kautsky. However, starting with the Russian Revolution of 1905 and the debates that followed—in Germany with the formation of an independent left wing of the SPD—the divorce with the "orthodox center" was inevitable. Kautsky's refusal in 1910 to publish an article by Rosa Luxemburg in *Die Neue Zeit* entitled "Was weiter?" (What next?) prompted the final break, both political and personal (although not with Luise!). Beyond this incident, which Rosa and her friends considered as a declaration of war against the Marxist Left and a capitulation to the party leadership, the disagreements were even more profound: as Haupt so shrewdly observes, Kautsky's thinking never moved beyond the intellectual climate of the turn of the century—scientism, positivist rationalism, linear evolutionism, and social Darwinism.

The case of the Bolshevik leader is different, with a series of highs and lows, of theoretical polemics and political rapprochements. The correspondence reveals an abiding critique of the politics of the Mensheviks, accused of supporting the social patriots of the PPS in Poland, without however approving of their majority opponents in the RSDLP (Russian Social Democratic Labor Party), which appeared too "Blanquist." Nevertheless, in 1907, during the Congress of the Socialist International in Stuttgart, the alliance with Lenin enabled the Left to carry the day. The break occurred in 1912 due to Bolshevik support of the internal opposition that would go on to provoke a crisis at the heart of the SDKPiL.

The historical context and tone differs significantly in the correspondence from the final years, from 1914 to 1919, which Georges Haupt selected and assembled in the second volume published by Maspero, *J'était, je suis, je serai* (1977). These letters, insists the editor, are presented in their entirety and not redacted, censured, or amputated—like the correspondence with Sonia Liebknecht first published in 1920, which was watered down and drained of color. The historian begins by citing a passage drafted by Luxemburg herself several weeks before her assassination that sums up, in his view, her journey from August 4, 1914, to January 15, 1919: the revolution must climb "step by step, by degrees, the bitter Golgotha of its own experiences." The letters from this period, he explains, drafted under difficult circumstances, often behind prison bars, through years of disappointment and solitude but also ceaseless struggle, "count among the most beautiful specimens of the epistolary genre." It is no mistake, he adds, that they have been edited and reedited so many times, read and loved by multiple generations of socialists from 1920 to the present day.

Faced with the capitulation—all the more brutal for being unforeseen, indeed unforeseeable—of the entire Socialist International (or at least the great majority of it) in August 1914, Rosa Luxemburg was, as we know, among the few leaders of the SPD to refuse to give in to the spreading wave of nationalism and warmongering. The journal that she went on to found several months later with Karl Liebknecht and a few others had a title that was at once both a profession of faith and a program of action: *Die Internationale*. Her reflections lean toward an all-encompassing and heartrending questioning of hard-won certainties that would nevertheless remain unachieved. The letters bear witness not only to her lucidity and her firm and unflinching stand in the face of betrayal by the cynical and arrogant right wing of the SPD and the "cowardice" of the centrist "swamp," but also her passion for literature, art, nature, botany, and birds; they also contain an implicitly philosophical dimension, and the search for a worldly, humanist, socialist ethic.

Targeted for persecution by the authorities, vilified by her former friends, Luxemburg did not balk: she adapted to the challenging conditions of prison life "with an exemplary will and courage," Haupt observes, while citing this passage from one of her letters: "I will not allow myself to be demoralized." Where did this extraordinary capacity for resistance come from? She drew strength both from an ethical position and a philosophy of history, from, on the one hand, her choice to remain faithful to her commitment and the refusal to stoop to servility, and, on the other, her confidence in the "implacable laws of the dialectic of history," "the implacable laws of evolution." Naturally, this does not allow for passivity; what is needed, she wrote, is "not a passive patience but one that engages all of our energies."

This optimistic philosophy of history, this belief in the necessity of progress—the foundation of the whole early twentieth-century socialist worldview—was undoubtedly there in the correspondence and writings of Rosa Luxemburg. But I regret that Georges Haupt did not pay closer attention to the famous catchphrase of the *Junius Pamphlet: The Crisis of Social Democracy* (1915): "socialism or barbarism." This expression in my view constitutes a true turn in the history of Marxist thought: she opened a path toward an open conception of the historical process, where the "final goal," socialism, would no longer appear inevitable but simply one among multiple possibilities, such as barbarism. Rosa Luxemburg is here referring to a passage by Friedrich Engels, but in fact it is she who first formulated in the field of Marxism this vision of history as an unforeseeable process, crisscrossed with forks in the road.

News of the Russian Revolution of 1917 was received by the prisoner as an "elixir of life." Closely following the unfolding events, she greeted the October Revolution with enthusiasm: as Haupt observed, she supported and defended the revolution led by Lenin "with sympathy and anxiety." Both attitudes are present in the celebrated text drafted behind bars in the summer of 1918 and published by Paul Levi in 1922, *The Russian Revolution*. Haupt's commentary perfectly captures the spirit of this momentous document: "Few have so clearly perceived the historic impact of this revolution, and no one better understood the consequences of the absence of democracy, the despotism, the terror." In short, Haupt declares, the Bolshevik revolution enjoyed her full support, "but without beatific admiration."

Liberated from prison by the German Revolution of 1918–19, Rosa Luxemburg threw herself body and soul into the revolutionary vortex. Braving all dangers, having to permanently live in hiding, she went to fight her last battle. On January 5, Haupt recounts, she got caught up in the adventure, if not a trap per se, carried along by the dynamic of the revolution itself. We know the rest: on January 15, the arrest and assassination of Rosa Luxemburg and Karl Liebknecht by soldiers of the Freikorps (future breeding-ground of Nazism), mobilized by the rightist Social Democratic government of Ebert-Scheidemann. "She fell," Haupt writes with evident emotion, "on the field of honor, like the combatants from those days in June 1848, the victims of the Commune, which she often cited as an example."

Concluding this remarkable introduction from 1977—one of his last writings, which came out less than a year before his sudden death—Haupt quotes from Lessing, repeated by the founder of the Spartacus League in an article published in early 1919: "To teach the whole truth, or nothing at all, and to teach it clearly and frankly, without mystery, inhibition, or suspicion, but in all its power."

One could hardly imagine a better summary of the profession of faith of Georges Haupt as a historian of the international workers' movement.

Translated by Lynne Sunderman

8. Rosa Luxemburg and Trotsky

"Of all the personalities of European socialism, nobody was in origin, temperament and political and literary gifts more akin to Trotsky than Rosa Luxemburg."
—Isaac Deutscher, *The Prophet Armed*

Social Democracy assassinated Rosa Luxemburg in 1919. Stalinism, from 1925 on, wanted to purge the Comintern of this dangerous "syphilis" (in the words of Ruth Fischer, a leader of the German Communist Party), i.e., Rosa's ideas. Leon Trotsky, on the other hand, in 1935 joined her, with Lenin and Karl Liebknecht, as the three revolutionaries claimed by the embryonic Fourth International.

Despite their differences, the profound communion between Trotsky and Rosa Luxemburg stems from revolutionary Marxism and internationalist communism, of which they were both authentic and lucid representatives.

It is also, however, a communion marked by tragic combat against the pathological excrescence of the workers' movement as signified by its reformist bureaucracy, a combat which cost them both their lives (murders ordered by Noske in 1919, and Stalin in 1940) and witnessed the temporary triumph of the "gravediggers" of the revolution. [Gustav Noske, a right-wing Social Democrat, was minister of defense in the German Weimar Republic —Ed.*]

---

* Lynne Sunderman's English translation of this chapter was first published in *Against the Current* 214 (September–October 2021), accompanied by the editorial notes retained here.

We know that Trotsky and Rosa Luxemburg met only rarely. In *My Life*, Trotsky describes his impression of Rosa's character at one of these meetings, the conference of the Russian Social Democratic Labor Party (RSDLP) in 1907: "Short of stature, frail, even sickly, she had noble traits, eyes that gleamed with spirit, and could subjugate with the virility of her character and mind. Her style, strained, precise, implacable, will forever reflect her heroic spirit." Then he adds, revealing a certain regret, "I admired her from afar. And yet it may be that I never properly appreciated her."

Realistically speaking, despite their limited personal interaction, there is a remarkable similarity in young Trotsky's and Rosa's vision of the world, their methods, their strategic aims and political theories.

They are united by their weaknesses, their errors, and their insights. Among their errors, the most significant is undoubtedly their rejection of the Leninist theory of organization.[1] Here we can see Rosa's influence on the young Trotsky, who even mentions her explicitly in his pamphlet *Our Political Tasks* as an orthodox Marxist leader who had come out publicly against Lenin's centralism.

It is also around this time (1904) that Trotsky first met Rosa Luxemburg. In a discussion with Marceau Pivert in 1939, Trotsky freely admitted that in that pamphlet, he defended his "very similar views to those of Rosa Luxemburg" but stressed that his subsequent experience proved that "on this question, Lenin was correct, and Rosa Luxemburg and I were not."

Rosa and Trotsky's error was in not distinguishing between certain one-sided formulas found in *What Is To Be Done?* and the essence of the Leninist theory of the party: the strict, rigorous, centralized organization of the revolutionary vanguard, and political orientation of the proletariat.

After the 1905 revolution, in a new 1907 preface to *What Is To Be Done?*, Lenin admitted that the pamphlet contained a few "rather maladroit or imprecise" ideas.[2] Nevertheless, he worked tirelessly for fourteen years on this solid, tempered organization, this clandestine splinter group implanted in the factories which for the first time in history had paved the way for the proletarian revolution—the Bolshevik Party.

The roots of Rosa and Trotsky's misunderstanding of the Leninist theory of the party (revealed on a political level by their confused and conciliatory position between Mensheviks and Bolsheviks) can be found in what could be termed their "revolutionary catastrophism." Like Kautsky and most of the "orthodox" Marxists of the Second International, before 1914, Rosa and Trotsky believed that the fall of capitalism was inevitable and that the victory of the proletariat would be irresistible.

This "optimistic fatalism," this naive faith in the "iron laws of history," is the theoretical foundation of their semi-spontaneous organizational ideas, a foundation that was obviously quite shaken by the collapse of the Second International [over member parties' support of their own imperialist governments on the outbreak of world war —Ed.] in August 1914. It was no accident that precisely at the outset of World War I, Trotsky began to reconnect with the Bolsheviks.

Nevertheless, Rosa and the young Trotsky's organizational error did contain a rational basis: much earlier than Lenin, they recognized the threat of the rising power of the party apparatus, the conservative tendency toward the self-preservation of the organization (which ultimately became an end in itself)—in a word, the danger of bureaucratization.[3]

Rosa Luxemburg had understood earlier than Lenin the profoundly reformist bureaucratic character of the German Social Democratic Party instrument and its official "orthodox Marxist" ideologue, Karl Kautsky, whereas the young Trotsky had already demonstrated by 1906 in his *Results and Prospects* a sense that the conservatism of the Social Democratic parties of Europe (and of Germany in particular) could ultimately become "an obstacle in the proletariat's straightforward struggle for power."[4]

What Kind of Revolution?

Rosa's and the young Trotsky's profound intuition also revealed itself—well before Lenin's theses in April 1917—in the formulation of a strategy for the proletarian revolution in Russia. It appears that around 1905–6 the two arrived at similar conclusions, albeit by different routes on the character of the 1905 revolution, which was for them "not so much . . . the last successor of the old bourgeois revolutions as the forerunner of the new series of proletarian revolutions of the West."[5]

At the 1907 Russian Social Democratic Labor Party convention in London, Trotsky's speech on the Russian Revolution received Rosa and Leo Jogiches's wholehearted approval. According to Trotsky, that speech also led to a reconciliation between them and to their collaboration in Rosa's Polish journal *Prezeglad Socialdemokraticzny.*[6]

What's more, at the 1909 conference of the RSDLP, it was Rosa who gave the speech and led the majority to take up the maxim "the dictatorship of the proletariat supported by the peasantry," which was, incidentally, introduced by Trotsky in 1905.

It is for this reason that in 1931 Stalin included Rosa among the "inventors" of the "utopian project" of permanent revolution and in his papal bull entitled "Some Questions Concerning the History of Bolshevism" decided to "excommunicate" her posthumously for the sin of perpetuating Trotskyism.

One might well ask how Rosa and the young Trotsky were able to rationalize the coexistence of their organizational misunderstanding with their grasp of strategic truth. However, there may in fact be a paradoxical link between the two. Let us simply sketch out a possible hypothesis that only more in-depth research can confirm.

Before 1917, for both Rosa and Trotsky, the strategy of the Russian Revolution was articulated around two tightly linked axes: the hegemonic role of the proletariat and the extension of the revolution in Western Europe, particularly in Germany. These theories were founded on the following premises:

1) a remarkable analysis of the social forces in Russia and of the internal dynamic of the revolutionary process based on the 1905 model (with a certain underestimation of the peasantry, especially by Rosa);

2) Europe's economic and political unity (the premise of their mistaken conception of the national question); and

3) the revolutionary spontaneity of the European proletariat,
     which, spurred by the Russian Revolution, would rise up de-
     spite and against the Social Democratic parties (the premise
     of their organizational conception).

The two latter premises were the foundation of their hopes for, or
even their certainty of, a rapid extension of the Russian Revolution in
Europe, which they felt was actually key to proletarian victory in Russia itself. Thus their strategy for the Russian Revolution was based
both on correct assumptions (their analysis of Russian socioeconomic development, for example in Trotsky's *Results and Prospects*)
as well as on false premises, which were incidentally the exact source
of their political errors about the party and the national question.

In reality, as Trotsky subsequently recognized, the Russian proletariat, supported by the peasantry, was able to triumph and take power
without outside help from a revolution in Western Europe (although
naturally, it was not able to construct an isolated socialist society in
Russia). The two other premises were thus totally unnecessary.

One can thus see how, with regard to each problem, "error"
and "truth" were jumbled together in a complex and contradictory
combination.

Russian Revolution and After

In 1917, Lenin became "Trotskyist" (as Kamenev complained in 1917),
and Trotsky Leninist. Armed with the April Theses, the Bolshevik
Party led the Russian proletariat to power in October.

A few months later, even as she criticized various aspects of Bolsheviks' politics (to which we shall return presently) from her hiding place in Germany, Rosa Luxemburg sketched out a pamphlet in
which she offered her enthusiastic support to Lenin and Trotsky, two
names that were for her, as for any other revolutionary of the era,
completely inseparable.

Upon her release from prison thanks to the 1918 revolution,
Rosa decided not to publish her account, having changed her mind

on certain points. She had intended to rework the text, but her plans were tragically interrupted by reactionary executioners in service to the Social Democrat Noske.

Three months after this ignoble crime, Trotsky wrote in the first manifesto of the Communist International (March 1919) that "[w]e communists, united in the Third International, recognize the direct continuation of the efforts and heroic martyrdom in the long series of revolutionary generations, from Babeuf to Karl Liebknecht and Rosa Luxemburg."

It was not until 1932 that Trotsky "rediscovered" Rosa. The occasion was offered, so to speak, by Stalin, who, in the above-mentioned article ("Some Questions Concerning the History of Bolshevism"), accused Rosa of capitulating to opportunism because, unlike Lenin, she had not broken with Kautsky before 1914.

Trotsky easily destroyed this dishonest falsification with the aid of the famous letter from Lenin to Shlyapnikov from October 27, 1914: "I now hate and detest Kautsky most of all . . . R. Luxemburg was right; she understood long ago that Kautsky was only the lackey of the party majority, of opportunism."

He returned to this problem in 1935 in his article "Rosa Luxemburg and the Fourth International" to underscore that "Rosa Luxemburg understood and began much earlier than Lenin to combat how the ossified party machinery and the unions had served to put the brakes on the movement."

In reality, Trotsky "rediscovered" Rosa as he struggled against Stalinism, which had particularly sensitized him to the antibureaucratic dimension in Rosa's work, directed less against Lenin (with all due respect to certain anti-Leninists who claim to be Luxemburgists) than against that which then constituted the principal bureaucratic machine of the international workers' movement: the leading apparatus of the German Social Democratic Party, a bureaucracy against which she had struggled all her life and was responsible for her death in 1919.

Trotsky thus "rediscovered" Rosa Luxemburg as the bureaucracy of the Communist Party of the Soviet Union and the USSR deteriorated.

In 1932, as he struggled against Stalin's centralization via his polemic against Stalin's slanderous article, Trotsky "rehabilitated" Rosa and brought to light her critique of Kautsky's opportunistic centrism.

In 1935, he emphasized Rosa's opposition to the "[p]hilistines of opportunistic bureaucracy," and to the "crusty reformist apparatus" of the Second International. There was a striking resemblance between the Communist parties of 1935—a parliamentary opposition, verbally revolutionary, but in reality reformist and "moderate"—and German Social Democracy before 1914.

It was this resemblance (which is not to say identity), this problematic commonality, that explains Trotsky's renewed interest in Rosa, not to mention the growing understanding of his own struggles as the continuation of Rosa Luxemburg's—except that by 1917, Trotsky had definitively absorbed the essentials of the Leninist conception of the party into his own theoretical system, with the result that his defense of Rosa Luxemburg was not without reservation.

The moral of the story was that for Trotsky, "if we disregard the incidentals or that which has already been resolved by evolution, then we may fully expect to orient our work for the Fourth International under the sign of the '3 Ls,'" not only of Lenin but also of Luxemburg and Liebknecht.

With this solemn proclamation, beyond the falsifications and Stalinesque lies, Trotsky reconnected with the tradition of the Third International, during which it had been decided, since the death of Lenin in 1924, to commemorate the "3 Ls" in January. But for Trotsky, it was a question not of formal rehabilitation but rather of restoring the revolutionary vanguard to the precious heritage of Rosa Luxemburg's ideas, which for the most part belonged to the arsenal of revolutionary international communism.

The Debate Continues

In later times, we have witnessed diverse attempts to oppose Rosa Luxemburg to both Trotsky and Lenin. See for example Gilbert Badia, historian of the French Communist Party, in his otherwise interesting and well-documented work, as he gives way to the old demons of Stalinism: "We have found no identity, not even of convergence, in their respective theories. . . . Trotsky himself affirmed a kinship that does not exist between Rosa Luxemburg's ideas and his own."[7]

How then can we interpret, if not as a kind of convergence, the adoption by the 1908 conference of the Social Democratic Party of Poland (SDKPiL), headed by Rosa Luxemburg, of the slogan of the dictatorship of the proletariat and supported by the peasantry, put forward by Trotsky at the very same moment? We must send G. Badia back to read works by Isaac Deutscher (an author who has now been "rehabilitated" and cited by [French Communist journal] *France Nouvelle* . . .), who shows with precision the similarities in the approach of these two revolutionary Marxists.

On an altogether-different and less serious topic, the "new philosopher" André Glucksmann [a onetime Maoist who became a right-wing ideologue —Ed.] has been trying to put Rosa Luxemburg in the same camp with Alexander Solzhenitsyn for the benefit of his crusade against the "Bolshevik terror."[8]

In his polemic against Glucksmann, Daniel Singer humorously describes an imaginary meeting between R. Luxemburg and Solzhenitsyn:

> She could not be in the same room as Solzhenitsyn without pinching her nostrils, because he symbolized everything—the nationalism, the obscurantism of the Orthodox Church, the idealization of the peasantry, and the glorification of the past—all the vile stench of Holy Mother Russia, the knout, and the pogroms that she so detested. . . . And, based on Solzhenitsyn's criteria, what old goat is mangier than Rosa the Red, the revolutionary, the internationalist?[9]

Yes, Rosa Luxemburg criticized Lenin and Trotsky in her renowned pamphlet on the Russian Revolution, drafted in prison in 1918 and published after her death by Paul Levi. But her critique had nothing in common with that of the Social Democrat reformists (Kautsky and company) or of the liberal bourgeois, to say nothing of a partisan of the tsar-like Solzhenitsyn, to the extent that she is clearly situated in the same camp as the Bolsheviks, the October Revolution, and the revolutionary Marxists: "All the revolutionary honor and capacity for action which Western Social Democracy lacked were represented by the Bolsheviks. Their October uprising was not only the actual salvation of the Russian Revolution; it was also the salvation of the honor of international socialism."

At the conclusion of her text, she insists on the distinction between the essential and the nonessential in Bolshevik politics: what is essential is revolutionary coherence, and, proceeding from that, "the future everywhere belongs to Bolshevism."[10] What is secondary are tactical errors that she decries passionately but fraternally.

Rosa Luxemburg's polemical remarks partially correspond to a very questionable conception of the tactic of alliances, which today sparks mainly historical interest: for example, her rejection of the slogan about the right of self-determination, or her opposition to the Bolsheviks' agrarian policies ("The Land to the Peasants").

Her position on the Constituent Assembly (whose dissolution by the Bolsheviks in 1918 she criticized) had by all appearances changed after the revolution in November 1918 in Germany and the emergence of the Workers' Councils. In her last articles from 1918–19, she seems to have considered the power of the Workers' Councils as contradictory to a Constituent Assembly.

The key question of democratic socialism remains unanswered: Rosa Luxemburg's criticisms of the Bolsheviks have lost none of their urgency. On the contrary, they appear in fact prophetic in that they attracted attention to the dangers of policies that severely restricted democratic liberties as instituted by revolutionary powers in Russia:

> Without a free and untrammeled press, without the unlimited right of association and assemblage, the rule of the broad masses of the people is entirely unthinkable. . . . Freedom only for supporters of the government, only for the members of one party—however numerous they may

be—is no freedom at all. Freedom is always and exclusively freedom for the one who thinks differently.[11]

Contrary to latter-day Eurocommunists, Rosa Luxemburg supported the dictatorship of the proletariat, but she stressed that it was "a dictatorship of the class, not of a party or clique—a dictatorship of the class, that means in the broadest public form, on the basis of the most active, unlimited participation of the mass of the people, of unlimited democracy." That is the historic mission of the proletariat: "by conquering political power, to create a socialist democracy to replace bourgeois democracy—not to destroy democracy altogether."[12]

Nevertheless, in the dramatic and almost untenable situation in which the Bolsheviks found themselves in 1917–18, surrounded by imperialists, threatened by White troops and foreign interventionists, how could they have done otherwise? Rosa Luxemburg responds to this pertinent objection in one of the most important passages of her entire pamphlet:

> It would be demanding something superhuman from Lenin and his comrades if we should expect of them that under such circumstances they should conjure forth the finest democracy, the most exemplary dictatorship of the proletariat and a flourishing socialist economy. By their determined revolutionary stand, their exemplary strength in action, and their unbreakable loyalty to international socialism, they have contributed whatever could possibly be contributed under such devilishly hard conditions. The danger begins only when they make a virtue of necessity and want to freeze into a complete theoretical system all the tactics forced upon them by these fatal circumstances, and want to recommend them to the international proletariat as a model of socialist tactics.[13]

How can we fail to recognize Rosa Luxemburg's clairvoyance and the justice of her critique? How, after sixty years of bureaucratic degeneration in the USSR, can we reject the vital necessity of an unlimited democracy to safeguard the power of the proletariat? It seems that the moment has come for Marxist revolutionaries to say clearly and out loud: on the chapter on socialist democracy, it was Rosa Luxemburg who got it right.

That was in fact the point of the document on "The Dictatorship of the Proletariat and Socialist Democracy" approved by the United Secretariat of the Fourth International in 1977.[14] Was that, then, not an adoption of Rosa's conception of freedom in a workers' state?

Translated by Lynne Sunderman

9. Notes on Lukács and Rosa Luxemburg

A dialogue with Rosa Luxemburg's thinking has a central place in Lukács's work in the period from 1917 to 1923. In this chapter we will try to sort through some of the main agreements and disagreements between them within a common theoretical and political framework.

Lukács discovered the work of Rosa Luxemburg in 1917–18. In his intellectual autobiography from 1933, "My Road to Marx," he recognizes that her prewar writings had a "powerful and lasting" impact on him.[1] Which readings is he speaking of? Quite likely *Reform or Revolution?* (1899), which would have resonated with his viscerally anti-reformist sensibilities, but especially *The Mass Strike, the Political Party, and the Trade Unions* (1906). Proof of this "powerful and lasting" impact is the fact that he had a Hungarian translation of *The Mass Strike* published in 1921, for which he wrote a clearly "Luxemburgist" preface.

In 1918, Lukács was directly influenced by Hungarian social historian and philosopher Ervin Szabó, whose romantic-revolutionary thinking was expressed in an anticapitalist trade unionism that was radically opposed to the moderate and parliamentary politics of Hungarian Social Democracy. An attraction to trade unionism was surprisingly characteristic of intellectual representatives of prewar anticapitalist romanticism. For Ferdinand Tönnies, trade unions were one of the chief methods to restore a sense of *Gemeinschaft* (community) at the heart of modern industrial society; Max Weber welcomed the unions' "idealism" compared with Social Democratic "platitudes"; his friend Robert Michel, whom Friedrich Naumann described at the time as a "romantic revolutionary," organized an anti-parliamentary unionist current in Germany; similar trends connected with Georges Sorel and Hubert Lagardelle emerged in France, and in Italy with Arturo Labriola, etc.[2] From this perspective of romantic anticapitalism, Lukács reads *The Mass Strike, the Political Party, and the Trade Unions* along with revolutionary syndicalist writings by Sorel, Henriette Roland-Holst, and Szabó himself. In an autobiographical writing from 1967, he refers to the "contradictory amalgam" of Sorel, Szabó, and Rosa Luxemburg that characterized the political thinking of the period.[3] Nevertheless, it is likely that the writings of Rosa Luxemburg had a mediating effect for Lukács between revolutionary romanticism and Marxism that would ultimately lead him, in December 1918, to join the Hungarian Communist Party.

It was only later, around 1920, that Lukács would read Luxemburg's economic writings: the essay "The Marxism of Rosa Luxemburg" from January 1921 was the first to include references to *The Accumulation of Capital* and *Anti-Critique*. *Introduction to Political Economy* was published later, in 1925; thus, Lukács would not have been familiar with the part of Luxemburg's oeuvre that most clearly demonstrated its romantic dimension. One nevertheless finds here and there in his *History and Class Consciousness* an echo of analyses in *The Accumulation of Capital* on precapitalist communities but in a new theoretical framework: the theory of reification. Lukács emphasizes that reification is a "historic and transient" phenomenon produced by capitalism absent not only in the precapitalist past but also in the postcapitalist future: in primitive societies, one can still find a "non-reified structure," and thanks to socialist revolution "the prospect opening up of re-establishing non-reified relations between man and man and between man and nature."[4] A more appropriate translation of *Wiedererlangung*, the term used by Lukács to express the idea of "re-establishing," would be "reconquer," which clearly hearkens back to a revolutionary romantic vision, which Lukács and Rosa Luxemburg shared, of socialism's reestablishment of a lost dimension from the past.

In *History and Class Consciousness*, Lukács examines Rosa Luxemburg's thought in three chapters: "The Marxism of Rosa Luxemburg" (January 1921), "Critical Observations on Rosa Luxemburg's 'Critique of the Russian Revolution'" (January 1922), and "Towards a Methodology of the Problem of Organization" (September 1922). Between the first and the two last essays, we will observe a significant change in Lukács's thinking about Rosa Luxemburg, a change that we will endeavor to explain in the context of its concrete historical framework. In the chapter "The Marxism of Rosa Luxemburg," Lukács is mainly concerned with the methodological and political social aspects of Luxemburg's economic writings (especially *The Accumulation of Capital*), aspects which he passionately defends against the "vulgar Marxism" of her critics (Otto Bauer, etc.). Taking as his point of departure the central thesis of *The Accumulation of Capital*, that unlimited capitalist accumulation is impossible, Lukács then deduces "the theoretical certainty of the coming social revolution."[5] This problem of the inevitable socialist revolution (for economic reasons) is also characteristic of Luxemburg's writings from before 1914; given the catastrophe of the workers' movement due to the war, however, Rosa Luxemburg in the *Junius Pamphlet* formulates the question in more open and dialectical terms: the economic and political crisis of capitalism will lead either to socialism or barbarism. Social revolution is not a priori a "theoretical certainty" but rather an objective possibility. We will see that Lukács's own position on this subject will also evolve in this direction after 1921.

The idea of a decisive link between economic crisis and revolutionary explosion for Lukács is illustrated in the form of the following thesis, which he attributes to Rosa Luxemburg:

> For the active and practical side of class consciousness, its true essence, can only become visible in its authentic form when the historical process imperiously requires it to come into force, i.e. when an acute crisis in the economy drives it to action. At other times it remains theoretical and latent, corresponding to the latent and permanent crisis of capitalism.[6]

Lukács finishes this remark with the following note: "Rosa Luxemburg, *Mass Strike*." However, Luxemburg's thesis in this work is remarkably different. For her, it is not economic crisis but revolutionary political praxis that transforms latent to active consciousness: "when the masses themselves appear on the political battlefield this class consciousness becomes *practical and active*."[7]

We therefore see in Lukács a profoundly "economic" articulation of Luxemburg's ideas. This reappears in the following passage when he attributes to Luxemburg an economic theory of spontaneity of which he wholeheartedly approves:

> The form taken by the class consciousness of the proletariat is the Party. Rosa Luxemburg had grasped the spontaneous nature of revolutionary mass actions earlier and more clearly than many others. (What she did, incidentally, was to emphasise another aspect of the thesis advanced earlier: that these actions are the necessary product of the economic process.) It is no accident, therefore, that she was also quicker to grasp the role of the party in the revolution.[8]

This passage calls for several remarks:

1. For Rosa Luxemburg, revolutionary spontaneity was not necessarily the result of an "economic process." In *The Mass Strike, the Political Party, and Trade Unions*, she shows how the massive and spontaneous worker revolt in Petrograd had begun as an act of solidarity (with workers fired for belonging to a union) that, after the massacre by the tsar's troops, was transformed into "a revolutionary declaration of war on absolutism."[9]

2. The theory according to which mass actions are essentially spontaneous effectively come from Rosa Luxemburg. It remains to be seen who these "many others" are who could not understand this spontaneous feature and the role of the party in the revolution. Was it Lenin? In this essay, Lenin is only mentioned once, as the brilliant author of *The State and*

Revolution. It seems rather that she is referring to Kautsky, Bebel, etc.; in any case, it is clear that Lukács identifies much more strongly with the Luxemburgist theory of the party than with Leninism.

This identification is particularly salient in the following remark: "Rosa Luxemburg perceived at a very early stage that the organization is much more likely to be the effect than the cause of the revolutionary process."[10] From this typically Luxemburgist idea Lukács deduces another that perhaps goes beyond the spirit of Rosa's writings: "The correct slogans give rise organically to the premises and possibilities of even the technical organization of the fighting proletariat."[11]

We will see that most of these organizational designs are explicitly criticized in the two other essays of the book in which Rosa's theory of the party is discussed. In a curious note at the bottom of a page drafted in 1922 that followed immediately after the remark on the role of the party in the revolution, Lukács distances himself from Rosa's ideas: "On the limitations of her view see the essays 'Critique of the Russian Revolution' and 'Towards a Methodology of the Question of Organization.' In the present essay we are only concerned to present her point of view."[12] Far from merely presenting her point of view, Lukács unreservedly and ardently adopts the perspective of Rosa Luxemburg, who "recognized earlier and more clearly than others" the spontaneity of mass movements, the role of the party, the concept of organization as a product of action (*l'organisation-produit*),* etc.

We know that several of the essays in *History and Class Consciousness* were profoundly reworked based on Lukács's evolving opinions on various political and methodological problems. The question that emerges is this: Having radically changed his position regarding Rosa Luxemburg's theory of the party (as illustrated in the last two essays of *History and Class Consciousness*), why did Lukács not decide

---

* *L'organisation-produit* refers to an organizational model based on: multidisciplinary teams who are responsible for their product, a culture of trial and error, a user-centric product that is constantly evolving. —Ed.

to rework his essay "The Marxism of Rosa Luxemburg"? Or even better: Why did he not add a note explaining that by 1922 he had moved beyond his views from January 1921? Why, against all evidence, did he claim that his essay was merely a neutral "exposition" of Rosa Luxemburg's views? We must admit that there is no clear answer to these questions. The fact remains that regarding the theory of the party of Rosa Luxemburg, *History and Class Consciousness* contains two contradictory positions, which might strike one as rather odd given that the work itself is generally characterized by its remarkable coherence.

Sometime in 1921 there appeared a Hungarian edition of Rosa Luxemburg's *Mass Strikes* (1906) with an introduction from Lukács. In all likelihood it was drafted around the same time as the essay "The Marxism of Rosa Luxemburg" because in it he defends totally analogous positions, i.e., a warm and unreserved adherence to the ensemble of Rosa Luxemburg's economic and political works. Lukács's organizational ideas, or rather his "reading" of Luxemburg's ideas, evolved with regard to mass strikes. According to Lukács, this type of strike develops "as an inevitable consequence of economic development" and is not at all a momentary, organized act prepared in advance. Thus, "organization is not a premise but the consequence of mass strike and thus of revolution. The *Communist Manifesto*'s assertion that through revolution the proletariat will organize itself as a class was clearly confirmed by the Russian Revolution."[13] The term "Russian Revolution" in this text refers exclusively to the revolution of 1905–7, which is the topic of Luxemburg's pamphlet. It is significant that Lukács's essay nowhere mentions the October Revolution, a fact that is difficult to explain given his socioeconomic framework of interpretation.

On the key question of "spontaneity," the positions expressed in Lukács's introduction for the most part correspond with those of Luxemburg's pamphlet, which he coherently and systematically defends.

The change in Lukács's attitude on Luxemburg's organizational conceptions occurred not in 1922 but well before, a few months after the essay from January 1921 ("The Marxism of Rosa Luxemburg"). In two articles published in the journal *Die Internationale* (the theoretical journal of the German Communist Party), around May–June of 1921, for the first time, Lukács criticized these ideas on behalf of the party's Leninist theory.

The historical framework of this polemic is the "March Action of 1921," the failed attempt of the German Communist Party to launch a general attack starting with a strike in the mining region of Mansfield. The action was criticized as an adventurist undertaking by one wing of the party (Clara Zetkin, Paul Levi, which got the latter excluded) and passionately defended by the majority of the Central Committee (Ruth Fischer, Maslow, etc.). Lukács wholeheartedly adopts the position of the leaders of the German Communist Party and in his two articles sharply criticizes the tactical positions promoted by the minority. And since Clara Zetkin referred to certain texts by Rosa Luxemburg (particularly *Mass Strikes*) to describe the tactics of the party leaders as "putschist," Lukács suddenly found himself in the position of disagreeing with Luxemburgist ideas.

In the first of these articles, "Spontaneity of the Masses, Activity of the Party" (*Die Internationale*, III/6, 1921), he plainly asserts that the debate at the heart of the German Communist Party is nothing but a return to the old confrontation from 1904 between Rosa and Lenin on the subject of the Russian party's organizational issues.[14] He does not deny the value of Luxemburg's ideas on mass strikes, but he insists that they are conceptions that correspond to the stage of bourgeois revolution. In the acute stage of the proletarian revolution, relations between the party and the masses is no longer what Luxemburg was talking about in 1906: a simple "acceleration" of a spontaneous movement which would ultimately be achieved independently of the party. This presupposes a "necessary and irresistible [*swangsläufig*]" development of revolutionary action according to "natural laws" that the party must recognize and use "exactly as in technology in which the laws of nature are properly studied for use in the natural sciences."[15]

According to Lukács, the "natural laws" of the economy produce nothing but crisis and not its socialist outcome; this requires the conscious action of the proletariat. If the proletariat is paralyzed by revisionism, by Menshevik ideology at heart, the crisis could unleash "the common fall of classes in struggle back into a state of barbarism."[16] The expression "the common fall of classes in struggle" comes from the Communist Manifesto. The historic alternative between socialism and barbarism was clearly articulated by Rosa Luxemburg in her *Junius Pamphlet* (1915). Therefore, Lukács's critique is only valid in some sense for Rosa's writings from 1906, or at least before 1914. In reality, Lukács himself underwent a political evolution not unlike Rosa Luxemburg's: from a certain revolutionary fatalism to a more dialectical vision of socialist revolution as a historical possibility. Thus, far from breaking with Luxemburgism on this issue, Lukács merely passed from Rosa's positions from 1906 to those of 1915.

Why this sudden turn in Lukács in April–May 1921? For Rosa Luxemburg, it was spurred by a historical worldwide catastrophe, the capitulation of the labor movement in response to bourgeois nationalism. For Lukács, it was evidently the failure of the March Action that prompted a theoretical revision as well as an abandonment of the "fatal optimism" that was still apparent in his essay from January 1921. In hindsight, the event seems relatively secondary; at the time, however, it was a major event that unleashed a fierce debate, not only in Germany but also in all of Europe and the USSR, to the point that it became the central theme of the Second Congress of the Communist International. We can nevertheless ask precisely why it was the failure of the March Action of 1921, rather than the defeat of the Hungarian Commune of 1919, that was the main motive for the shift in Lukács's thinking. Perhaps because Lukács (much like Lenin?) considered Germany as key to the destiny of European and worldwide revolution?

In the second article, "Organizational Questions on the Revolutionary Initiative" (*Die Internationale* III/8, 1921), Lukács continued to defend the tactics of the German Communist Party leadership. The failure of the March Action can be explained by the lack of discipline (that is, in a spiritual, ideological/moral sense rather than administratively speaking) and centralization in the Communist Party. In this context, Lukács returns to his charge against Rosa Luxemburg's theories on organization, arguing that her main error in 1904 was in not comprehending the true sense of Lenin's propositions: in rejecting centralism and the discipline of the Bolshevik model, she was left with the structure of the old Social Democratic parties of central Europe. She had missed the heart of the new organizational design: the increased demands that militantism implies, rigorous ethical demands on each member that required their total engagement in the party.[17]

These two essays thus illustrate the moment that Lukács embraced the Leninist theory of the party and his rupture with Rosa Luxemburg's organizational theories. It is entirely characteristic of Lukács that it was the ethical dimension of Lenin's theories that became his "rallying point."

The irony of this situation is that Lukács backed Leninism (from an organizational standpoint) by way of an unconditional defense of the March 1921 Action and a critique of the ideas of Clara Zetkin, which he characterized as being Luxemburgist. For his part, however, Lenin severely criticized the adventurism of the German Communist Party leadership during the March Action and was rather in agreement with Clara Zetkin.

Must we then conclude that Lukács's Leninism was not shared by Lenin himself? It would appear that beyond the errors of 1921, from the March Action onward, Lukács sets himself squarely within the bounds of Bolshevik organizational ideology. That said, it is clear that that includes a peculiar conception of Leninism, which, along with his polemic against Rosa Luxemburg, he develops in *History and Class Consciousness*.

During the year 1922, Lukács wrote the last two chapters of *History and Class Consciousness*. One of these chapters is a direct confrontation with Rosa Luxemburg's text on the Russian Revolution (published in 1922 by the expelled leader of the German Communist Party, Paul Levi); the other is a methodological debate on the problem of the party, with a critical analysis of Rosa Luxemburg's theories. One can study these two texts as a relatively homogeneous pair.

In 1922, Lukács had not yet renounced his unreserved adherence to the economic theories of Rosa Luxemburg. In the preface to *History and Class Consciousness* (dated "Christmas 1922"), he proclaims categorically that Rosa Luxemburg, "alone among Marx's disciples, has made a real advance on his life's work in both the content and methods of his economic doctrines."[18]

Nevertheless, he no longer deduces from these facts "a theoretical certainty of the coming social revolution"; he instead begins to believe that socialism is an objective possibility that does not inevitably emerge from the crisis of capitalism; if the revolutionary proletariat does not succeed in overthrowing the bourgeoisie, the contradictions of capitalism can lead to barbarism.[19]

On the topic of organizational issues, Lukács undertakes a profound revision of Luxemburg's ideas from 1921. This does not, however, imply a total and dogmatic rejection but rather a nuanced and critical judgment that endeavors to integrate certain fertile ideas from Rosa Luxemburg within a fundamentally Leninist framework.

First of all, Lukács continues to believe that on the meaning of mass actions in general and on the 1905 revolution in particular, it was Rosa Luxemburg who had "the clearest view": "She locates the defects of the traditional notions of organization in its false relation to the masses."[20] In this context, it is clear that for Lukács, "the traditional notions" are those of the parties of Western Europe, particularly Germany, before 1914.

In another passage, Lukács again praises "her correct polemic against the mechanical forms of organization in the workers' movement as in, e.g. the question of the relationship between the party and the trade unions and between the organized and unorganized masses."[21] It thus appears that Lukács considers Rosa Luxemburg's critique of fixed and bureaucratic understandings of German Social Democracy as well as her insistence on the revolutionary potential of the unorganized proletarian masses as an achievement of the modern Marxist theory of the party. He goes even further and adopts as his own the Luxemburgist theory that in mass movements, rather than technical leadership, the task of the party is above all political leadership, an idea that he characterizes as "a great step forward in understanding the whole problem of organization."[22]

Nevertheless, within her "correct polemic" against the bureaucrats, according to Lukács, Rosa Luxemburg ends up with an "overestimation of spontaneous mass actions"; she did not appreciate that "the class consciousness of the proletariat does not develop uniformly throughout the whole proletariat, parallel with the objective economic crisis."[23] It would appear that this critique by Lukács stems from a certain misunderstanding. In 1922, Lukács continued to believe that the spontaneity of the masses is simply the result of economic crisis. According to him, the spontaneity of a movement, we note, is only the subjective, mass-psychological expression of its determination by pure economic laws.[24]

As we have seen, however, this "economic" theory is not at all Rosa Luxemburg's. Lukács believes that spontaneity has limits because it is simply the immediate result of economic crisis and criticizes Rosa Luxemburg for not understanding its limits. However, for Luxemburg herself, spontaneity is not necessarily the direct result of economic crisis. It has an essential political dimension, both in its causes and results at the level of class consciousness. In other words, Lukács's critique is irrelevant: if Rosa Luxemburg underestimated the spontaneity of the masses, it was an underestimation in any case not based on the premises to which Lukács ascribes it.

Yet another of Lukács's critiques appears questionable: according to Lukács, Rosa Luxemburg was of the opinion that "the working class will enter the revolution as a unified revolutionary body"; she disregarded the key fact that "large sections of the proletariat remain intellectually under the tutelage of the bourgeoisie";[25] in short, for Lukács, she underestimated the "terrible ideological crisis within the proletariat itself." It is in this context that Lukács brings up *The Mass Strike, the Political Party, and Trade Unions.* While this critique may be valid vis-à-vis the 1906 pamphlet, by 1915 it is not valid at all (the *Junius Pamphlet*), given that its central theme is precisely the "terrible ideological crisis" of the workers' movement. In fact, all of Luxemburg's writings from August 1914 on acknowledge the overwhelming fact of the ideological submission of vast sectors of the proletariat to bourgeois ideology: nationalist and militaristic until 1918 and then parliamentarist from November 1918 to January 1919.

On at least one important point, Lukács's critique of Rosa Luxemburg can be taken as a critique of his own positions in his essay from 1921: the Luxemburgist point that organization is something that proceeds organically as "a historical product of the class struggle," an argument that Lukács rejects in 1922 as being one sided.[26] Lukács's judgment is nevertheless nuanced: "Rosa Luxemburg saw very clearly that 'the organization must come into being as the product of struggle.' Her mistake was merely to overestimate the organic nature of the process while underestimating the importance of conscious organization."[27]

The most significant critique, however, which for Lukács constituted the crux of the debate with Lenin, was that Rosa Luxemburg conceived of political struggle against opportunism as a "difference of opinion" with no organizational consequences: "The conflict between them lay in their answers to the question whether or not the campaign against opportunism should be conducted as an *intellectual* struggle *within* the revolutionary party of the proletariat or whether it was to be resolved on the level of *organization*."[28]

While significant, Lukács's critique here is formulated in terms that are too vague to do justice to Rosa Luxemburg's positions. To be relevant, it would need to specify—which party, and in which period?

It appears undeniable that in 1904 Rosa Luxemburg had not yet grasped the inevitable organizational implications of the conflict between the revolutionary and Menshevik wings of the Russian Social Democratic Labor Party. With regard to the German Social Democratic Party after 1914, it is likely that Rosa Luxemburg and the German "radical Left" realized relatively late that an organizational rupture with opportunism was necessary. Nevertheless, in the prewar period in Germany, no one, particularly Lenin, believed that breaking with Kautsky and the centrist-opportunist leadership of Social Democracy. On the contrary, well before the Bolsheviks,

Rosa Luxemburg understood the ultimately reformist character of the "orthodox center" of the SPD.

It is not within the scope of this essay to examine Lukács's theory of the party in detail. Let us simply acknowledge that proceeding from a critical discussion of Rosa Luxemburg's arguments and employing a certain Luxemburgist problematic in *History and Class Consciousness*, Lukács constructs a particular version of Leninism.

Thus, for Lukács, organization must be based on "the interaction of spontaneity and conscious control": the party must escape from the dilemma of opportunism and terrorism; it must be neither a sect that acts for the "unconscious" masses, in its place and as its representative, nor a reformist organization that passively adapts to the momentary desires of the masses.[29]

Even Lukács's ideas on the internal structure of the party originate from both Lenin and Luxemburg. With regard to Lenin, Lukács underscores the absolute necessity of centralization, discipline, and especially the total engagement of every member, with one's whole self and existence, in the party's life.[30] With Rosa, he believes that it is necessary to abolish "the harsh unrelenting contrast between leader and the masses, that has survived as a vestige of bourgeois party politics."[31] He sees these two demands as not only not contradicting each other but actually dialectically connected: "Every decision of the party must result in actions by all the members of the party . . . in which the individual members risk their whole physical and moral existence. For this very reason they are not only well placed to offer criticism, they are forced to do so together with their experiences and their doubts."[32]

In our opinion, such a unique synthesis of the organizational ideas of Lenin and Luxemburg was only possible because the two camps are less incompatible than is generally assumed . . .

As we know, Rosa Luxemburg's pamphlet on the Russian Revolution was written from prison in 1918 and published by Paul Levi in 1922. Lukács's critical essay on this text (in *History and Class Consciousness*) is not only a defense and illustration of Bolshevism but indirectly continues the polemic against Paul Levi and the wing of the KPD opposed to the March Action.

Some of Lukács's critiques are difficult to challenge. His positions on the agrarian question (i.e., rejection of the partition of communal lands led by the Bolsheviks) and on the national question (i.e., rejection of the slogan of the right to self-determination) in particular show how Rosa Luxemburg underestimated the role and importance of nonproletarian elements in the revolution.[33]

In criticizing the Bolsheviks' dissolution of the Constituent Assembly in 1918 (to the advantage of the Soviets) in an article on the situation in Germany from December 1918, Rosa Luxemburg appears to have had a change of heart: "A constituent assembly or all power in workers' and soldiers' councils, the abandonment of socialism or the most resolute proletarian class struggle armed against the bourgeoisie: that is our dilemma."[34] Lukács's critical remarks on this topic demonstrate his insistence on the importance of the soviets, i.e., workers' and soldiers' councils, as a specific and necessary form of the proletarian revolution, as opposed to the structural forms of bourgeois revolutions, such as the National Convention of the French Revolution, etc.

The key question, however, naturally concerns the relationship between socialist democracy and the dictatorship of the proletariat. Unlike present-day Eurocommunists, Rosa Luxemburg was in fact in favor of the dictatorship of the proletariat, but she stressed that this must be:

> a dictatorship of the class, not of a party or of a clique—dictatorship of the class, that means in the broadest public form on the basis of the most active, unlimited participation of the mass of the people, of unlimited democracy . . . The historical task of the proletariat, once it comes to power, is to build socialist democracy in place of bourgeois democracy, not to abolish all democracy.[35]

Lukács categorically rejected the distinction between the party and class dictatorship, which in his view stem from "exaggerating utopian expectations" and "anticipating later phases in the process."[36] What does Lukács mean by this assertion? That class dictatorship could only be established "later on"? Rosa Luxemburg had already responded to this very argument in an ironic and lucid argument in her pamphlet:

> But socialist democracy is not something that begins only in the promised land after the foundations of socialist economy are created; it does not come as some sort of Christmas present for the worthy people who, in the interim, have loyally supported a handful of socialist dictators. Socialist democracy begins simultaneously with the beginnings of the destruction of class rule and of the construction of socialism. It begins at the very moment of the seizure of power by the socialist party. It is the same thing as the dictatorship of the proletariat.[37]

In Rosa Luxemburg's view, socialist democracy necessarily entailed liberty; as she wrote in one of the most renowned pages of this text:

> [W]ithout a free and untrammeled press, without the unlimited right of association and assemblage, the rule of the broad masses of the people is entirely unthinkable. . . . Freedom only for the supporters of the government, only for the members of one party . . . is no freedom at all. Freedom is always and exclusively freedom for the one who thinks differently.[38]

Lukács's response to this altogether-coherent claim is underwhelming and illustrates an act of faith. For Lukács, "freedom cannot represent a value in itself (any more than socialisation). Freedom must serve the rule of the proletariat, not the other way round."[39] This would require that the proletariat "reign" without freedom of press, association, and assembly, without political pluralism, and thus with no democratic control over its own representatives . . . Sixty years' of historical experience would seem to have largely confirmed the clairvoyant lucidity of Rosa Luxemburg's ideas and the decisive importance of democratic liberties for the very existence of proletarian power. Far from being "utopian," Rosa Luxemburg's approach was the only realistic one since she alone was able to guarantee the workers' state and the power of the soviets in the face of bureaucratic degeneration, that is, against the Stalinist golem, which, between 1935 and 1940, would be responsible for the deaths of the Bolsheviks of 1917 themselves.

While recognizing that the possibility of a "self-criticism performed by the proletariat—the possibility of which must be kept open institutionally even under the dictatorship,"⁴⁰ Lukács explains neither which institutions he is referring to nor just how the proletarian critique of revolutionary power could be exercised without democratic liberties. His reproach against "utopianism" appears even less well founded since Rosa Luxemburg was very well aware of the immense objective difficulties (civil war, foreign intervention, economic disorganization, famine, etc.) that the Bolsheviks faced and the need for emergency measures; in the conclusion of her pamphlet, she insists that

> [i]t would be demanding something superhuman from Lenin and his comrades if we should expect of them that under such circumstances they should conjure forth the finest democracy, the most exemplary dictatorship of the proletariat and a flourishing socialist economy. By their determined revolutionary stand, their exemplary strength in action, and their unbreakable loyalty to international socialism, they have contributed whatever could possibly be contributed under such devilishly hard conditions. The danger begins only when they make a virtue of necessity and want to freeze into a complete theoretical system all the tactics forced upon them by these fatal circumstances, and want to recommend them to the international proletariat as a model of socialist tactics.⁴¹

This passage, incidentally, reveals the shallowness of those who since 1922 have tried to turn this pamphlet into an ideological war machine against Bolshevism.

Translated by Lynne Sunderman

10. Ideology and Knowledge in Rosa Luxemburg

Toward the turn of the twentieth century, positivism in its diverse forms became the dominant ideology in Europe (and elsewhere, particularly in Latin America) in academia but also among politicians, the military, and entrepreneurs. It also penetrated deep into the belief system of the workers' movement, permeating what became known as "the Marxism of the Second International."

According to Lelio Basso, in his remarkable introduction to the correspondence between Kautsky and Rosa Luxemburg, "Scientism, rationalism, positivist naturalism, and Darwinist evolutionism are the core components of today's reasoning, and it is this ambiance that provides the cultural background for followers of Marxism."[1]

The influence of positivism on the intellectuals, leaders, and ideologues of German Social Democracy is revealed in two ways: (a) in its close complementarity with a neo-Kantian trend that favored ethical socialism (for example, in Bernstein), and (b) in its connection to a neo-Darwinist naturalism which was rather anti-Kantian (in Kautsky). We will show how these two tendencies, beyond their very real distinctions, are situated on a common terrain, and how Rosa Luxemburg attempted to move beyond their positivist aspects.

The crucial questions for situating the methodological challenges of this debate concern the relations between scientificity and the class struggle, between the perspective of the social classes and the objectivity of knowledge (in the social sciences).

Can Marxism simultaneously be a revolutionary doctrine that expresses the (political, social, moral, etc.) ideology of a class as well as a scientific theory that aspires to objective truth? Can it be a social science free from value judgments and ideological presuppositions, situated outside the class struggle?

Positivist conceptions of social science exist at the very heart of Bernstein's theoretical reflections. With his characteristically disarming sincerity, in an autobiographical text from 1924 he recognizes that "[m]y way of thinking rather predisposes me to a positivist philosophy and sociology."[2]

The methodological foundation of Bernstein's thinking is a remarkably articulated combination between Kant and Comte. For Bernstein, it is a question on the one hand of dismantling scientific socialism—the dialectical synthesis of science and revolution—into a "socialist ethic" inspired by the eternal principles of justice and Kant's categorial imperative (a concept defended by a number of neo-Kantian intellectuals who were in some way connected to Social Democracy: H. Cohen, P. Natorp, C. Schmidt, L. Woltmann, K. Vorländer, etc.). On the other hand, it is an economic and social science that is at once empirical, objective, and positivist. Bernstein thus separates value judgments (ethics) from judgments of fact (the positivist scientific approach), a separation demanded by both positivism and Kantianism, which were supposedly "confused" or "mixed" by Marx.[3]

With this conception of science as his point of departure, Bernstein criticizes Marx's partisan and biased thinking. In a letter to Bebel from October 20, 1898, he maintains that "*Capital*, with all its scientificity, was in the final analysis a tendentious work that remained unfinished, in my opinion precisely because the conflict between scientificity and partisanship made Marx's task ever more problematic."[4] A similar critique appears in his acclaimed *Preconditions of Socialism* from 1898, in which he insists on the contradictory character of Marx's approach, which "claims to elevate socialism to the level of science but subordinates the demands of science to a political tendency."[5] According to Bernstein, this duality is illustrated even at the heart of *Capital*, between analyses that are "exempt from prejudice" and those, particularly on the socialist "end goal," in which Marx relinquishes his scientific approach and becomes the "prisoner of a doctrine."[6]

In a conference from 1901, Bernstein goes further, casting doubt on the very possibility of scientific socialism: "Socialism as a science makes claims to knowledge, but socialism as a movement is guided by self-interest." For Bernstein, to the extent that interest and knowledge are mutually exclusive, these two requirements are strictly incompatible. "Science cannot be biased. In terms of knowledge of what is, science belongs to no class and no party." How can socialism, the doctrine of a party that is intended to be the expression of class interest, be scientific? Bernstein thus proposes replacing the term "scientific socialism" with "critical socialism" (in the Kantian sense). Knowledge of social phenomena, according to Bernstein, pertains not to socialism but to "scientific sociology . . . whose object, society, is a living organism" (a formulaic expression typical of a certain positivistic biologism that runs throughout university sociology from that period, from Spencer to Durkheim). This sociology must be as ideologically neutral as the natural sciences, which, for Bernstein as well as positivism in general, served as an epistemological model: "No one these days would speak of liberal physics, socialist mathematics, or conservative chemistry. Can the science of human history or human behavior be any different? I cannot accept that position, and I consider the idea that social science can be liberal, conservative, or socialist to be absurd."[7]

Kautsky's position is more contradictory but never manages to escape Bernstein's epistemological field. As Lelio Basso points out, "[H]is Marxism was in reality filtered through an evolutionist mentality with Darwinian origins and through a so-called scientific objectivism."[8] Like the positivists, Kautsky tends to equate nature with society, writing for example that social laws can be defined as natural laws "because in essence they are indistinguishable"; both society and nature "confront man as all-powerful forces with laws from which he cannot escape."[9] It logically follows then that the social sciences are but "one particular field of the natural sciences."[10]

With such premises as these, how does one approach the question raised by Bernstein and the neo-Kantians on the relationship between value judgments and judgments of fact in Marx's oeuvre?

In his work *Ethics and the Materialist Conception of History* (1906), Kautsky aims to respond to neo-Kantian ideas and to defend Marx from revisionist critiques. From the outset, however, he generally situates himself within Bernstein's positivist problematic, albeit while judging Marx's "objectivity" more sympathetically. Like Bernstein (and the positivists in general), he accepts the necessity of strictly separating value judgments (or "the moral ideal," "ethics," etc.) from judgments of fact. For Kautsky, scientific socialism includes no "ideal"; it is simply "scientific research on the laws of evolution and the movements of the social organism," (a typically social Darwinist description, incidentally). Under such conditions, the presence of the socialist ideal or of revolutionary ideology even at the heart of Marxist theory is conceived of as nothing more than human weakness, a psychological shortcoming, excusable and understandable certainly but necessary to overcome in order to attain true scientific knowledge:

> Naturally, in socialism the seeker is often also a combatant, and man does not allow himself to be artificially split in two. Thus, for example, Marx's scientific research at times reflected a moral ideal, although, to the extent that he was able, he always tried to eliminate it, and rightly so, because in science, a moral ideal becomes a source of error if it influences one's aims.[11]

In this passage three "classic" themes from positivism emerge: (1) ideology can only be a detriment to the process of attaining knowledge; (2) ideology can be eliminated from society's scientific knowledge; (3) its elimination is a question of effort, of "will" on the part of the seeker.

Furthermore, while defending Marx, Kautsky ends up adopting a position that is not so far removed from Bernstein's; for the latter, as we have seen, in his doctrine, Marx was now and again a victim of his own "bias." Kautsky also recognized that Marx had at times revealed his "ideals." The only difference is that Kautsky insisted on the "effort" that Marx made to overcome this disruptive element. The evidence, however, shows Kautsky in the weaker position in this debate since a reading of *Capital* clearly shows that Marx never made any attempt to "expunge" the ideological, politico-moral options or the revolutionary socialist tendencies from his scientific works. The neo-Kantians, those partisans of "ethical socialism," easily pointed out the plethora of value judgments throughout the three volumes of *Capital* by measuring him against the positivist yardstick of an ideological neutrality of the natural-scientific type. Kautsky had to accept (if only implicitly) the Bersteinian critiques. Where he was able to distinguish himself from his revisionist adversary, however, was in the question of the relationship between knowledge and social class. Contrary to Bernstein, Kautsky did not reject the link between social science and class struggle; in a very interesting passage from *Ethics and the Materialist Conception of History*, he goes so far as to propose that the perspective of the dominant class (with its own ideological and moral dimensions) could promote a scientific understanding of society: " In a society crisscrossed by class antagonism, a new scientific knowledge . . . generally implies an infringement of the interests of certain classes. Discovering and disseminating scientific knowledge that goes against the interests of the dominant classes is for them tantamount to a declaration of war."[12]

How can we reconcile this view with the aforementioned perceived need to "expunge" value judgments ("the moral ideal") from scientific work? Kautsky attempts to escape this contradiction via an ingenious albeit rather incoherent solution: in the paragraph following the above citation about the scientist who aims to serve the oppressed classes, he adds: "But even this last wish has a misleading tendency if it does not play a simple negative part, as repudiation of the claims of the ruling conceptions to validity . . . but wishes instead to rise above that and to take the direction laying down certain aims which have to be attained through social knowledge."[13]

From Kautsky's thesis here arise two fundamental objections:

1. If the role of the perspective of the growing oppressed class, i.e., that by virtue of its rejection of dominant bourgeois doctrines, the proletariat can only play a strictly negative role in knowledge, how does this pure negativity distinguish itself from that of other social classes that also reject the bourgeois *Weltanschauung*? We know that at the beginning of the nineteenth century, Germany experienced a romantic anti-capitalist trend, one of whose incarnations was "feudal socialism," which Marx spoke of in the *Manifesto*. Why then would Marx's theory be more scientific than Adam Müller's or Friedrich Karl von Savigny's (to say nothing of Joseph de Maistre or Louis de Bonald), since they both also rejected the liberal-bourgeois conception that was dominant throughout the nineteenth century?

2. Is knowledge of society in Marx's oeuvre not entirely devoted to a single precise goal—the emancipation of the proletariat and the establishment of socialism? Does the study of the economic laws of capitalism and its rigorous and objective scientific analysis not aim precisely to discover the conditions for the possibility of its abolition? And does the analysis of the bourgeois state not have as its stated goal its destruction? To be consistent, like Bernstein Kautsky should challenge the essence of Marx's work as "biased." What's more, does non-Marxist social science not also serve (whether consciously or unconsciously, directly or indirectly) specific aims linked to the interests of certain social classes?[14]

In his 1927 compendium, *The Materialist Conception of History*, Kautsky presents a more coherent approach in that he explicitly affirms that "as pure scientific doctrine, the materialist conception of history is in no way linked to the proletariat."

This idea is in no way exclusive to Kautsky: other representatives of the "orthodox Marxist" current in German Social Democracy also insist on the separation between judgments of fact and value judgments, and by extension between science and Marx's socialist ideology. For example, Rudolf Hilferding, in the preface of his *Finance Capital* (1910), explicitly states that it is

> false to suppose . . . that Marxism is simply identical with socialism. In logical terms Marxism, considered only as a scientific system, and disregarding its historical effects, is only a theory of the laws of motion of society. . . . [A]cceptance of the validity of Marxism, including a recognition of the necessity of socialism, is no more a matter of value judgment than it is a guide to practical action.[15]

An even more radical version of this approach is found in some of Max Adler's writings, according to which "Marxism is in its very essence nothing but pure science. . . . Like all science, Marxism is totally neutral [*völlig unpolitisch*], in the sense of taking a political stand."[16]

One of the only Marxist authors—if not the only one—in prewar Germany to question the very foundations of the dominant positivist or semi-positivist problematic and to advance certain points for discussion toward another conception of the relationship between knowledge and the social classes was Rosa Luxemburg.

It is true that Rosa Luxemburg never presented her views on this question in a systematic fashion and never wrote any text that developed her methodological views in a specific manner; nevertheless, her various remarks on the subject sprinkled throughout her work little by little reveal a "watermark" that is clearly distinguishable from other patterns competing for the theoretical field of German Social Democracy. A comparison of her critique of Bernstein with Kautsky's, developed during the same time period, is instructive.

Luxemburg's antirevisionist pamphlet from 1899, *Reform or Revolution?*, sketches out a radical critique of scientism, which claims to be above party and class:

> For Bernstein does not like talk of "party science," or to be more exact, of class science, any more than he likes to talk of class liberalism or class morality. He thinks he succeeds in expressing human, general, abstract science, abstract

liberalism, abstract morality. But since the society of reality is made up of classes which have diametrically opposed interests, aspirations and conceptions, a general human science in social questions, an abstract liberalism, an abstract morality, are at present illusions, pure utopia. The science, the democracy, the morality, considered by Bernstein as general, human, are merely the dominant science, dominant democracy and dominant morality; that is, bourgeois science, bourgeois democracy, bourgeois morality.[17]

Thus, for Rosa Luxemburg, moral and political ideologies as well as the social sciences are inevitably engaged in class struggle. The science of society is necessarily linked to the perspective and interests of a given social class, and it is only in a future classless society that one can imagine a nonpartisan, "universally human" social science. In distinguishing between the social and natural sciences, Rosa Luxemburg frees herself from the positivistic pledge while avoiding the trap of the flagrant ideologicalization of the natural sciences.

For Luxemburg, this admission does not simply beg the question; in her *Introduction to Political Economy*, she shows how, in a concrete social science, "the paths of bourgeois and proletarian knowledge already diverge" on all questions, including those which on first sight appear abstract and indifferent to social struggle: the contrast between the global economy and "national economy," between the historical method and the naturalist method, etc.[18]

This does not mean, however, that bourgeois scholarship cannot lead to important scientific outcomes. Rosa Luxemburg highlights the value of the scientific discoveries of the founders of political economy (Quesnay, Boisguillebert, Adam Smith, Ricardo), who dared to reveal capitalism in its "classical nakedness," and she contrasts the "scientific discoveries" of the great ancestors over the "inchoate brew of garbage" of contemporary bourgeois imitators.[19]

She insists even more on the value of certain romantic economists such as Sismondi, stressing his "supreme lucidity," "profound understanding of the real contradictions in the movement of capital," and "his profound perception of historical connections." It is emblematic of Rosa Luxemburg's attitude toward economic romanticism that she considered an intellectual like Sismondi, whose work is permeated with a nostalgia for a precapitalist past, as in some ways usurping Ricardo himself: "Sismondi also demonstrates his superiority over Ricardo in relation to a third important point: in contrast to the latter's crudely blinkered vision, in which no other forms of society exist apart from the bourgeois economy, Sismondi represents the broad historical horizon of a dialectical approach."[20]

In reality, the whole of Rosa Luxemburg's *Accumulation of Capital* is founded on "rehabilitating" and critically moving beyond economic romanticism, particularly from Sismondi, incidentally by drawing inspiration from remarks by Marx himself, who, in his theories on surplus value, emphasized how, contrary to Ricardo, Sismondi was "profoundly conscious of the contradictions in capitalist production," even if he remained a *laudator temporis acti* [one who praises the past].[21] Let us add that Rosa Luxemburg defended Sismondi against Lenin, whose contemptuous criticism of economic romanticism struck her as narrow minded and unjust.[22] That said, Rosa Luxemburg naturally never questioned the fact that Marx's work essentially grew out of a confrontation with the great classical economists, who were linked to a thriving bourgeoisie, in particular Ricardo himself.

Rosa Luxemburg saw the relationship between Marx and his "classical" predecessors as a complex and contradictory bond simultaneously marked by continuity and rupture. It was not a question of an "epistemological break" between purely ideological thought (the classicists) and Marx's "science" (see Althusser) but of moving beyond the limits of bourgeois science by the "spokesmen for the modern proletariat," who "drew their most deadly weapons" from discoveries made by Smith and Ricardo.[23] In other words, "The laws of capitalist anarchy and its future downfall that Marx brought to light are certainly a continuation of the political economy that was created by bourgeois scholars, but a continuation whose final results stand in very sharp contrast to the points of departure on this."[24]

This partial continuity between Marx and bourgeois political economy implicitly introduced a key problem for Marxist epistemology:
the relative autonomy of the science of society in relation to the social
classes. We shall return to this later.

How was Marxism able to bring about this *Aufhebung* (con-
servation–negation–leaving behind) of bourgeois science? Marx's
thought represents "the historical standpoint of the working class
in the fields of philosophy, history, and economics"; Marxists are,
ultimately, the ideologues of the working class.[25] For Rosa Luxemburg (as for Lenin), the term "ideology" was not, as it was for the
young Marx of *German Ideology*, a synonym of a false and reversed
image of reality, but simply a way to describe in its most meaning-
ful structures a form of thought that was linked to the perspective
of a social class; thus, it is not contradictory, either with regard to
science or to real knowledge.

According to Luxemburg, "[T]here is a special bond between
political economy as a science and the modern proletariat as a
revolutionary class." It is because Marx took the point of view of
the revolutionary proletariat and its socialist ideology, because he
found himself at a "higher vantage point" (*höheren Warte*) that in
his scientific analysis of capitalism, he was able to "perceive the limits of bourgeois economic forms."[26] Rosa Luxemburg's topological
metaphor here is particularly fortunate because it allows us to see
the difference between Marx's science and that of bourgeois economists not as a division between the pure light of science and ideological shadows but between two observatories, two promontories,
two mountains with varying elevations (though facing the same
landscape), each with its own field of visibility, its own horizon, the
higher one naturally with a longer view that goes beyond the limits
of the lower levels. This metaphor also allows us to perceive how a
bourgeois economist could discover a certain number of scientific
truths from within the field of visibility defined by their ideological
horizon, from within the theoretical space structured by their own
class perspective (whether consciously or not). While economic science is in no way reducible to its social and ideological bases, that is

what determines the limits of knowledge situated in a certain class perspective.

Furthermore, Rosa Luxemburg's image here paves the way for an understanding of concrete historical conditions that explains the advent of Marxism and its place in the evolution of economic science: not as the miraculous fiat lux of an individual genius, but as the scientific expression from the point of view of a new class, that of the modern proletariat, which sparks the sudden appearance of a "higher vantage point," and which creates the objective possibility of a vaster and more advanced awareness of social reality.

Naturally, it remains to be seen why there exists an epistemological superiority from the perspective of the proletariat, why Marxism is seated at a higher level of scientific comprehension. In her polemic with Bernstein, Rosa Luxemburg furnishes us with several elements for a coherent response to these questions:

1   The difference between Marx and Ricardo or Smith is not simply located on the level of responses to common questions, but at a much higher level: the questions and problems themselves are novel in Marx's work.

2   What allows Marx to pose these new questions and thus to "decipher the hieroglyphics" of capitalist economy is his historicist approach, his perception of the historical limits of capitalism, his ability to move beyond the naturalist and unchanging approach of the classics.

3   It is because of his socialist-proletarian perspective that Marx was able to realize the transitory and perishable character of capital, which was invisible in the bourgeois theoretical field.

4   Far from being at odds with knowledge of truth, socialist ideology and the perspective of the proletariat promotes the scientific understanding of society.

Scientific socialism results from the indissoluble dialectical unity between these two dimensions.[27]

Using Rosa Luxemburg's remarks as a point of departure, one could sketch out a parallel between the superiority of the classical political economy to feudal economic doctrines and that of Marx to bourgeois economists: in both cases, the point of view of the revolutionary class (the bourgeoisie of the eighteenth and beginning of the nineteenth centuries, the proletariat beginning in the middle of the nineteenth century) promoted a deeper and more scientific knowledge of economic and social reality by moving beyond the conservative and historical conceptions of the ideologues of the established order.

We should point out, however, that for Rosa Luxemburg, the relationship between science and the proletariat presents a peculiar characteristic that is specific to the proletariat as a revolutionary class: "because . . . a clarification [*Aufklärung*] of the laws of development was necessary to the class struggle of the proletariat, this struggle fertilized [*befruchtend gewirkt*] the field of social science, and the monument of this spiritual proletarian culture is Marx's doctrine."[28] Unfortunately, Rosa Luxemburg does not develop this potentially very rich and important idea, which could enable us to perceive the unique nature of the relationship between the working class and scientific truth: contrary to the revolutionary bourgeoisie, which was lifted to power by the "spontaneous" development of capitalism, the proletariat can only triumph in its struggle by conscious action that implies an objective awareness of social reality.[29]

Since the time of Max Weber, bourgeois social science has always accused Marxism of refusing to apply the same analysis of its own epistemological status, to use on itself the same cutting theoretical instruments used to expose its adversaries: historical materialism, the theory of class ideology, etc.

This is not a baseless reproach with regard to certain currents represented by Kautsky and other partisans of a Marxism that was supposedly "purely scientific"—if not "apolitical" (Max Adler!), but it does not apply to Rosa Luxemburg, who consciously aimed to shed light on the social and historical conditions of Marxism and who in fact proposed to apply the Marxist method to Marx's own work. Thus, after insisting on the historicity of social, economic, political, and ideological phenomena, she was led to pose the question of the historical limits of Marxism itself; bourgeois intellectuals, she wrote with some irony, have long searched in vain for a way to move beyond Marxism but do not realize that the only real way is found at the heart of the Marxist doctrine itself: "Historical to the end, it only claims to be valid for a limited time. Dialectical to the end, it carries within itself the certain seeds of its own decline." In concrete terms, Marx's theory corresponds to a period determined by economic and political development: the passage from the capitalist to the socialist stage of human history.[30] Only once communism is carried out and social classes have disappeared will we be able to go beyond the intellectual horizons represented by Marxism.

It is interesting to recall in this context the passage of *Reform or Revolution?* in which Rosa Luxemburg affirms, in contrast to Bernstein, that a general human science in social questions is "for the moment an illusion, a pure utopia."[31] The expression "for the moment" suggests that in a classless society, the possibility exists of a social science without ideological references and without a class perspective. In this science of communist society, the problem of the objectivity of knowledge is couched in radically new terms.

This thesis on the historicity of Marxism is taken up later by other Marxist thinkers, notably Lukács and Gramsci. In his *Prison Notebooks*, Gramsci stresses that the philosophy of praxis "sees itself historically, as a transitional stage of philosophical thought."[32] It is hard to know whether Gramsci was directly inspired by the writings of Rosa Luxemburg, but the similarity of their problematic is undeniable.

Althusser, who rejected this historicist approach and characterized its supporters (Rosa Luxemburg as well as Gramsci and Lukács) as "theoretical ultra-leftists," is condemned to backsliding into the positivist problematic; his "epistemological split" between science and ideology demands not only that he deny the link between Marx's science and his socialist ideology, but that he insist that Marx's science, like all science (social or natural: he makes no distinction) must "escape . . . the common fate of a singular history: that of the 'historic bloc' of the unity of structure and superstructure."[33]

It appears that it is only by starting with a dialectical and historicist conception of itself (as Rosa Luxemburg laid out) that historical materialism can become a method that coherently explains diverse forms of ideology, thought, and social knowledge, a method that makes no exception and does not place itself at the margins of historico-social totality. Any other conception can only result in the displacement of the science of society in general, and of Marxism in particular, from the historical process and global social movement.

Translated by Lynne Sunderman

Editor's Note and Acknowledgments

It has been a genuine pleasure to help make available the writings of my friend Michael Löwy on Rosa Luxemburg. And there are many who must be thanked for helping this book come into being—first, obviously, being Michael himself, whose research and writing created these essays, but who played an active role in helping to pull the book together and oversee its production. The translators making these writings available to a broader English-speaking readership are: Lynne Sunderman, Dan La Botz, Paul Le Blanc, an anonymous translator for *International Viewpoint*, and Nathan Legrand (who was able to check several of our translations).

The foreword for this volume comes from another dear friend, Helen C. Scott, with whom I have joined forces in helping to edit some of the works of Rosa Luxemburg herself. This includes the still-ongoing Verso project *The Complete Works of Rosa Luxemburg*, supported by the Rosa Luxemburg Foundation and overseen by an editorial board headed by the remarkable Peter Hudis.

The publication of this book has been made possible through the combined forces of Haymarket Books (headed by Anthony Arnove) and the International Institute for Research and Education in Amsterdam (particularly Alex de Jong). Of course, both Anthony and Alex work in concert with much-larger collectivities whose intellectual and manual contributions have been essential. In addition, fundraising efforts drew an even broader range of contributors, inspired by a sense of kinship and comradeship for the author and the subject of this volume.

Among the earliest of Michael's writings that I encountered (back in 1981) is the opening essay, published here under the title

"Rosa Luxemburg's Conception of 'Socialism or Barbarism.'" This essay has continued to resonate, also inspiring controversy and further exploration—including from another friend, ecosocialist activist Ian Angus, whose two important contributions in 2014 made it a focal point (published on John Riddell's blog *Marxist Essays and Commentary*): "The Origin of Rosa Luxemburg's Slogan 'Socialism or Barbarism'" and "Following Up on Luxemburg and 'Socialism or Barbarism.'"* I believe Michael's other contributions in this collection will also provide stimulus for continuing discussions and explorations, for years to come, among engaged scholars and committed activists.

Readers might also be interested in this general assessment of Michael's work in the online journal *Links: International Journal of Socialist Renewal*: "Open Marxism and the Dilemmas of Coherence: Paul Le Blanc's Reflections on the Contributions of Michael Löwy."†

The source for the essays produced in this book, most immediately, was a collection from France: Michael Löwy, *Rosa Luxemburg, l'etincelle incendiaire* (Montreuil: Le Temps des Cerises, 2019). The collection contained items appearing in a number of revolutionary periodicals (those in English including *Against the Current, Bulletin in Defense of Marxism, International Viewpoint*, and *New Politics*). Three items are first appearing, in their current form, in the present volume: "Revolution and Freedom," "Western Imperialism against Primitive Communism," and "Rosa Luxemburg and Internationalism."

---

* Available at https://johnriddell.com/2014/10/21/the-origin-of-rosa-luxemburgs -slogan-socialism-or-barbasism/ and https://johnriddell.com/2014/11/21/following -up-on-luxemburg-and-socialism-or-barbarism/.

† Published September 8, 2013; available at http://links.org.au/open-marxism -and-dilemmas-coherence-paul-le-blancs-reflections-contributions-michael-Löwy.

Notes

Foreword

1. For details see Ankica Čakardić, "From Theory of Accumulation to Social-Reproduction Theory," *Historical Materialism* 25, no. 4 (2017): 37–64.
2. Michael Löwy, "The Hammer Blow of the Revolution," this volume, chapter 3.
3. Paul Frölich, *Rosa Luxemburg: Ideas in Action* (London: Pluto, 1972), 56.
4. Frölich, *Rosa Luxemburg*, 224.
5. Michael Löwy, "Western Imperialism against Primitive Communism," this volume, chapter 5. See Hamid Dabashi, "Rosa Luxemburg: The Unsung Hero of Postcolonial Theory," *On Edward Said: Remembrance of Things Past* (Chicago: Haymarket, 2020), 195–99.
6. Michael Löwy, "The Spark Ignites in the Action," this volume, chapter 2.
7. Michael Löwy, "Revolution and Freedom: Rosa Luxemburg and the Russian Revolution," this volume, chapter 4.

1. Rosa Luxemburg's Conception of "Socialism or Barbarism"

All quotations in this chapter cited from a non-English source translated by Paul Le Blanc.

1. Cf. Georg Lukács, *History and Class Consciousness* (Cambridge, MA: MIT Press, 1971), 39.
2. Paul Frölich, *Rosa Luxemburg* (New York: Monthly Review Press, 1972), 222. [According to Greek mythology, Ariadne was a woman who gave a ball of thread to the Athenian hero Theseus; with this thread he would be able to find his way out of the labyrinth that contained the murderous, cannibalistic Minotaur. —Trans.]
3. Cf. the article by Bernstein in defense of the neo-Kantian Karl Vorländer and against the "folly" of the leftist Anton Pannekoek, in *Dokumente des Sozialismus* 3 (1903): 487.

4. Rosa Luxemburg, "Reform or Revolution," in *Rosa Luxemburg Speaks*, Mary-Alice Waters, ed. (New York: Pathfinder, 1970), 73.

5. Luxemburg, "Reform or Revolution," 39, 41.

6. Luxemburg, "Reform or Revolution," 60.

7. Kautsky had in his youth been an ardent disciple of Darwin, and still in his last work, *The Materialist Conception of History* (1927), he proclaims that his goal is to find the laws that are common "to the evolution of humans, animals and plants." Cf. Erich Mathias, "Kautsky und der kautsky-anismus," [Kautsky and Kautskyism] *Marxismusstudien* 2 (1957): 153.

8. Karl Kautsky, *The Road to Power* (Chicago: Samuel A. Bloch, 1909), 50. Cf. also the Erfurt Program of the German Social Democratic Party (1891), drafted by Kautsky and presenting socialism as a "naturnotwendiges Ziel," a goal resulting from "natural necessity."

9. Discussion at the 1907 Congress of the International at Stuttgart, in Lelio Basso, "Introduzione," in *Rosa Luxemburg, Scritti Politici* (Rome: Riuniti, 1967), 85.

10. Article of 1913 by Rosa Luxemburg, against Kautsky's "strategy of attrition," in Frölich, *Rosa Luxemburg*, 143.

11. Rosa Luxemburg, "The Junius Pamphlet: The Crisis in the German Social Democracy," in *Rosa Luxemburg Speaks*, 269. [This translation has been modified somewhat on the basis of Löwy's own translation. —Trans.]

12. Frederick Engels, *Anti-Dühring* (New York: International Publishers, 1966), 174, our emphasis. Cf. also 183: "[I]ts own productive powers have grown beyond its control, and, as with the force of a law of Nature, are driving the whole of bourgeois society forward to ruin or revolution."

13. Karl Marx, "Difference between the Democritean and Epicurean Philosophy of Nature," in Karl Marx and Frederick Engels, *Collected Works*, vol. 1 (New York: International Publishers, 1975), 44. According to Lukács, in *History and Class Consciousness* (79), the revolutionary consciousness of the proletariat appears precisely under the conceptual form of an *objective possibility*.

14. Cf. Basso, "Introduzione," 48.

15. In 1915, Rosa's faith in the future of humanity consequently appeared somewhat like the Pascalian wager: risk, possibility of failure, hope of success, in a "game" in which one engages one's life for a transcendent value. The difference with Pascal, of course, being: (a) the content of that value, and (b) its objective foundation for Rosa Luxemburg. On this subject see Lucien Goldmann, *The Hidden God* (London: Routledge & Kegan Paul, 1964), 300–302, which compares the

Pascalian wager with the Marxist wager.

16. On this subject see Michael Löwy, "From the Great Logic of Hegel to the Finland Station of Petrograd," *Critique* 6 (Spring 1976). [In the April Theses of 1917, Lenin indicated the need for the Russian Revolution not to pause at its bourgeois-democratic stage but to be transformed into a proletarian-socialist revolution. This constituted a dramatic shift in Lenin's thinking and a bold challenge to Russian Marxist "orthodoxy." —Trans.]

17. Leon Trotsky, *Our Political Tasks* (London: New Park, 1980), 123, our emphasis.

18. In Isaac Deutscher, ed., *The Age of Permanent Revolution: A Trotsky Anthology* (New York: Dell, 1964), 79.

19. Luxemburg, "Junius Pamphlet," 330.

20. Karl Liebknecht, "A Rosa Luxemburg—Remarques à propre de son projet de thèses pour le groupe 'Internationale'" [To Rosa Luxemburg—Remarks on her thesis project for the 'Internationale' group], *Partisans* 45 (January 1969): 113.

2. The Spark Ignites in the Action
The Philosophy of Praxis in the Thought of Rosa Luxemburg

All quotations in this chapter cited to a non-English source translated by International Viewpoint.

1. Karl Marx, *Early Writings* (Harmondsworth: Penguin, 1975), 422.

2. Karl Marx and Friedrich Engels, *The German Ideology*, in *Marx-Engels Collected Works*, vol. 5 (New York: International Publishers, 1976).

3. Isabel Loureiro, *Rosa Luxemburg: Os dilemmas da acao revolucionario* [The dilemmas of revolutionary action] (Sao Paulo: UNESP, 1995), 23.

4. Rosa Luxemburg, "Reform or Revolution," in *Rosa Luxemburg Speaks*, Mary-Alice Waters, ed. (New York: Pathfinder, 1970), 83.

5. Luxemburg, *Rosa Luxemburg Speaks*, 118.

6. Rosa Luxemburg, *Organizational Questions of the Russian Social Democracy* (London: Integer Press, 1934), 130, 128.

7. Rosa Luxemburg, *The Mass Strike, the Political Party, and the Trade Unions* in *Rosa Luxemburg Speaks*, 171–72.

8. Luxemburg, *Mass Strike*, 199.

9. Luxemburg, *Mass Strike*, 200.

10. Luxemburg, *Mass Strike*, 200, 198.

11. Karl Liebknecht, "À Rosa Luxemburg: Remarques à propos du projet

de theses pour le group 'Internationale'" [To Rosa Luxemburg—Remarks on her thesis project for the 'Internationale' group], *Partisans* 45 (January 1969.

12. Rosa Luxemburg, *The Junius Pamphlet: The Crisis of German Social Democracy* in *Rosa Luxemburg Speaks*, 269.

13. Friedrich Engels, *Anti-Dühring: Herr Eugen Dühring's Revolution in Science* (New York: International Publishers, 1966), 174.

14. Luxemburg, *Junius Pamphlet*, 269.

15. Loureiro, *Rosa Luxemburg*, 123.

16. Rosa Luxemburg, *The Russian Revolution* (1918), Bertram Wolfe, trans. (New York: Workers Age Publishing, 1940), available at http://www.marxists.org/archive/luxemburg/1918/russian-revolution/index.htm.

17. Georg Lukács, *History and Class Consciousness* (London: Merlin Press, 1971), 39, 43.

18. Lukács, *History and Class Consciousness*, 284.

19. Loureiro, *Rosa Luxemburg*, 321.

20. Rosa Luxemburg, *Our Program and the Political Situation* (1918), Dick Howard, trans., in *Selected Political Writings of Rosa Luxemburg* (New York: Monthly Review Press, 1971), available at http://www.marxists.org/archive/luxemburg/1918/12/31.htm.

3. The Hammer Blow of the Revolution

All quotations in this chapter cited to non-English sources translated by Dan La Botz.

1. Walter Benjamin, *Paris, capitale du XIXème siècle: Le Livre des Passages* [Paris, capital of the nineteenth century: The book of passages], Paris: Du Cerf, 2000), 681.

2. Georg Lukács, *Histoire et conscience de classe* [History and class consciousness] (1923) (Paris: Editions de Minuit, 1960), 48.

3. Rosa Luxemburg, *Réforme ou Révolution?* [Reform or revolution?] (1898), Irène Petit, trans., in *Œuvres*, vol. 1 (Paris: Maspero, 1978), 39. See also Rosa Luxemburg, *Reform or Revolution* in *Rosa Luxemburg Speaks*, Mary-Alice Waters, ed. (New York: Pathfinder, 1970) for a somewhat different translation of the quotations here and throughout this chapter.

4. Luxemburg, *Réforme ou Révolution?*, 43.

5. Luxemburg, *Réforme ou Révolution?*, 67–68.

6. Luxemburg, *Réforme ou Révolution?*, 43.

7. Luxemburg, *Réforme ou Révolution?*, 67.

8. Luxemburg, *Réforme ou Révolution?*, 70.

9. Rosa Luxemburg, *Réforme ou Révolution?*, 43

10. Rosa Luxemburg, *Le Socialisme en France, 1898–1912* [Socialism in France, 1898–1912] (Paris: Belfond, [1971]), 196, 228.

11. Rosa Luxemburg, "Social-démocratie et parlementarisme" [Socialism and parliamentarism] (1904), in *L'Etat bourgeois et la Révolution*, Carlos Rossi, ed. (Paris: La Brèche, 1978), 25, 29, 34–36.

12. Luxemburg, "Réforme ou révolution ?," 42.

13. Luxemburg, "Réforme ou révolution ?," 41.

14. Luxemburg, "Réforme ou révolution ?," 41.

15. Rosa Luxemburg, "Le revers de la médaille" [The flip side] (April 1914), in *L'Etat bourgeois et la Révolution*, 41.

16. Rosa Luxemburg, "Martinique" (1902), *Gesammelte Werke* vols. 1–2 (Berlin: Dietz Verlag, 1970), 250–51.

17. Rosa Luxemburg, "Die Akkumulation des Kapitals" [The accumulation of capital] (1913), *Gesammelte Werke*, vol. 5 (Berlin: Dietz Verlag, 1990), 318–19.

18. Luxemburg, "Die Akkumulation des Kapitals," 344, 350.

19. Luxemburg, "Reforme ou Revolution?," 77.

20. Luxemburg, "Reforme ou Revolution?," 78.

21. Luxemburg, "Reforme ou Revolution?," 44.

22. Voir à ce sujet l'Avertissement d'Emile Bottigelli dans Karl Marx, *La Lutte de Classes en France 1848–1850* [Class struggle in France, 1848–1850], (Paris: Editions Sociales, 1948), 9–20.

23. Luxemburg, "Reforme ou Revolution?," 75–76.

24. Rosa Luxemburg, "Grève de masses, parti et syndicat" [The mass strike, the political party, and the trade unions] (1906), Irène Petit, trans., in *Œuvres*, vol 1., 127–28, 154.

25. Rosa Luxemburg, "Notre programme et la situation politique" [Our program and the political situation] (1918), Irène Petit, trans., in *Œuvres*, vol. 1, 106–8.

26. Luxemburg, "Reforme ou Revolution?"

27. Rosa Luxemburg, "The Russian Revolution," in *Rosa Luxemburg Speaks*, Mary-Alice Waters, ed. (New York: Pathfinder Press, 1970), 393.

4. Revolution and Freedom
Rosa Luxemburg and the Russian Revolution

1. J. P. Nettl, *Rosa Luxemburg*, abridged ed. (London: Oxford University Press, 1969), 435.

2. Paul Frölich, *Rosa Luxemburg*, Jacqueline Bois, trans. (Paris: Maspero, 1965), 299. Quotation translated into English by Michael Löwy.
3. This and all subsequent quotes, except where otherwise noted, are from Rosa Luxemburg, *The Russian Revolution*, Bertram Wolfe, trans. (New York: Workers Age Publishers, 1940), available at https://www.marxists.org/archive/luxemburg/1918/russian-revolution/.
4. *Batrachomiomachia*, "war between frogs and mice," is an allegory of Greek origin, describing a parodic and ridiculous confrontation between pseudo-opponents.
5. Frölich, *Rosa Luxemburg*, 303.
6. Quoted in Daniel Guérin, ed., *No Gods, No Masters* (Oakland, CA: AK Press, 2005), 391–92.

5. Western Imperialism against Primitive Communism
A New Reading of Rosa Luxemburg's Economic Writings

All quotations in this chapter cited to non-English sources translated by Michael Löwy.

1. Rosa Luxemburg, *The Accumulation of Capital*, Agnes Schwarzschild, trans. (London: Routledge & Kegan Paul, 1951).
2. The copy we're referencing here has a curious history. It is a selection of writings by Rosa Luxemburg published by the "Marx-Engels-Lenin-Stalin Institut beim ZK der SED," with a preface by Wilhelm Pieck, the Stalinist leader of the German Democratic Republic, followed by introductions of Lenin and Stalin, emphasizing the various "errors" of the Jewish/Polish/German revolutionary. This copy was purchased in a used bookshop in Tel Aviv and it had a handwritten dedication with the following words: "Sorry, we couldn't find an edition of R.L. Works without these superfluous 'introductions.' With kindest regards, Tamara and Isaac. Throttle Green, 25 August 1957." Obviously, the authors of the inscription were Tamara and Isaac Deutscher.
3. Rosa Luxemburg, "Einführung in die Nationalökonomie" [Introduction to economics] (1909), in *Ausgewählte Reden und Schriften*, 2nd ed. (Berlin: Dietz Verlag, 1955), 513. As Ernest Mandel notes in his preface to the French translation, "[T]he explanation of the fundamental differences between an economy based on the production of use values, destined to satisfy the needs of production, and an economy based on the production of goods, takes up most of the book." Ernest Mandel,

"Preface," in Rosa Luxemburg, *Introduction à l'économie politique* [Introduction to political economy] (Paris: Anthropos, 1970), xviii.

4. Luxemburg, "Einführung," 580. There exists an English translation of parts of the *Introduction to Political Economy* in a US-published 400-page *Rosa Luxemburg Reader* (New York: Monthly Review Press, 2004), edited by Kevin B. Anderson and Peter Hudis. Hudis is also the author of an interesting essay on the non-Western World in Rosa Luxemburg writings, which focuses mainly on the differences between her and Marx on the Russian rural community. See Peter Hudis, "Accumulation, Imperialism, and Pre-Capitalist Formations: Luxemburg and Marx on the non-Western World," *Socialist Studies / Études socialistes* 6(2) Fall 2010: 75-91.

5. Luxemburg, "Einführung," 501.

6. Luxemburg, "Einführung," 584, 601.

7. Luxemburg, "Einführung," 523.

8. Luxemburg, "Einführung," 634.

9. Luxemburg, "Einführung," 509.

10. Luxemburg, *Accumulation of Capital*, 376, 380.

11. Luxemburg, *Accumulation of Capital*, 370.

12. Luxemburg, *Accumulation of Capital*, 371.

13. Luxemburg, *Accumulation of Capital*, 371, 380, 384.

14. Luxemburg, *Accumulation of Capital*, 403.

15. Luxemburg, "Einführung," 525.

16. Luxemburg, "Einführung," 525, 661.

17. Gilbert Badia, *Rosa Luxemburg, journaliste, polémiste, révolutionnaire* [Rosa Luxemburg, journalist, polemicist, revolutionary] (Paris: Editions Sociales, 1975), 498, 501.

18. Luxemburg, "Einführung," 632.

19. Luxemburg, "Einführung,"585–86.

20. Luxemburg, "Einführung," 621. "With the Russian village community, the eventful destiny of primitive agrarian society reached its end; the circle was closed. In the beginning a spontaneous [*naturwüchsiges*] product of social evolution, the best guarantee of a society's economic progress and material and intellectual prosperity, the agrarian community [*Markgenossenschaft*] became an instrument of political and economic regression. The Russian peasant being whipped by members of his own community in the service of tsarist absolutism is the cruelest historical criticism of the narrow limits of primitive communism and the most striking expression of the fact that the social form itself is also subjected to the dialectical rule: reason becomes

nonsense, benefits become afflictions [*Vernunft wird Unsinn, Wohltat Plage*]." Peter Hudis discusses the discrepancy between Luxemburg's critical view of the Russian community and the more favorable approach of Marx in his letter to Vera Zassulitsch (1881). See Peter Hudis, "Neue Einschätzungen zu Rosa Luxemburgs Schriften über die Nich-Westliche Welt" [New assessments of Rosa Luxemburg's writings on the non-Western world], in Narihiko Ito et al., eds., *China entdeckt Rosa Luxemburg* (Berlin: Dietz Verlag, 2004).

21. Luxemburg, "Einführung," 575.

6. Rosa Luxemburg and Internationalism

All quotation in this chapter cited to non-English sources translated by Lynne Sunderman.

1. Isaac Deutscher, *The Non-Jewish Jew: And Other Essays* (London: Oxford University Press, 1968), 26, 27, 40.

2. Rosa Luxemburg, *J'étais, je suis, je serai! Correspondance 1914–1919* [*I was, I am, I shall be! Letters 1914–1919*], Georges Haupt, ed. (Paris: Maspero, 1977), 13. Luxemburg is referring to the genocide of the Herrero people of South West Africa by German colonial troops under the command of General Lothar von Trotha. The original text can be found in *Das Menschliche entscheidet: Briefe an Freunde* (Munich: P. List Verlag, 1958), 13. See also Georg Adler, Peter Hudis and Annelies Laschitza, eds., *The Letters of Rosa Luxemburg* (London: Verso, 2011), 376, which provides a slightly different translation.

3. Review of a pamphlet by the Bund published by Rosa Luxemburg in *Przegląd Socjaldemokratyczny* 4, no. 4 (1903): 159–63, quoted in Robert S. Wistrich, *Revolutionary Jews from Marx to Trotsky* (London: Harrap, 1976), 80.

4. Rosa Luxemburg, quoted in Wistrich, *Revolutionary Jews*, 84–85. The Black Hundred were a tsarist paramilitary group often implicated in pogroms.

5. Gustav Noske, quoted in Wistrich, *Revolutionary Jews*, 89. Noske, who was head of military affairs in the SPD-led government, organized the quashing of the January 1919 Sparticist Uprising by calling on the extreme rightist Freikorps, which would go on to assassinate Rosa Luxemburg and Karl Liebknecht.

6. Rosa Luxemburg, "Affaire Dreyfus et cas Millerand" [Dreyfus affair and the Millerand case] (1899), in *Le socialisme en France, 1898–1912*, Daniel Guérin, ed. (Paris: Belfond, 1971), 82.

7. Until 1917, Poland was a province of the tsarist Russian Empire.
8. See Michael Löwy, "Le problème de l'histoire (remarques de théorie et de méthode)" [The problem of history (remarks on theory and method)], in Georges Haupt, Michael Löwy, and Claudie Weill, eds., *Les marxistes et la question nationale (1848–1914)* (Paris: L'Harmattan, 1997), 375–78.
9. Rosa Luxemburg, *Internationalismus und Klassenkampf, Die polnische Schriften*, Jürgen Hentze, ed. (Berlin: Luchterhand, 1971), 192, 217.
10. Rosa Luxemburg, *Die Russische Revolution* [The Russian Revolution] (Frankfurt am Main: Europäische Verlanganstalt, 1963), 60.
11. Georg Lukács, *History and Class Consciousness* (Cambridge, MA: MIT Press, 1971), 27, originally published in German as *Geschichte und Klassenbewusstsein, Studien über marxistische Dialektik* (Berlin: Malik Verlag, 1923), 39, 41.
12. Rosa Luxemburg, *L'Accumulation du Capital* [The accumulation of capital] (1913), in Œuvres complètes, vol. 5, Marcel Ollivier and Irène Petit, trans. (Marseille and Toulouse: Agone & Smolny, 2019), 377.
13. J. P. Nettl, *Rosa Luxemburg* (London: Oxford University Press, 1966), 296–97.
14. Rosa Luxemburg, "Martinique", *Gesammelte Werke* (Berlin: Dietz Verlag, 1970), 250–51.
15. Luxemburg, *L'Accumulation du Capital*, 280, 281, 285.
16. Luxemburg, "Unser Kampf um die Macht" (1911), *Gesammelte Werke* (Berlin: Dietz Verlag, 1972), 537.
17. Luxemburg, "Kleinbürgerliche oder proletarsche Weltpolitik?" [Petty-bourgeois or proletarian world politics?], in *Gesammelte Werke*, 29.
18. Rosa Luxemburg, *Introduction to Political Economy*, in *The Complete Works of Rosa Luxemburg*, vol. 1, *Economic Writings I*, Peter Hudis, ed. (London: Verso, 2013), 156.
19. Luxemburg, *Introduction to Political Economy*, 157, 162.
20. Rosa Luxemburg, *Introduction à l'Economie Politique* (Paris: Anthropos, 1970), 138–142, 155.
21. Luxemburg, *Introduction* à l'Economie Politique, 80. Despite Rosa Luxemburg's validation of the communal village structure, she is well aware of the existence of the despotic power and privileged castes of pre-colonial India, which undergirded relations of exploitation and inequality.
22. Luxemburg, *Introduction* à l'Economie Politique, 92.
23. Luxemburg, *Introduction* à l'Economie Politique, 81.
24. Rosa Luxemburg, *L'Accumulation du Capital*, 385. The geographer David Harvey has recently reiterated the notion of capitalism's "permanence of primitive accumulation (accumulation by dispossession)."

See David Harvey, *The New Imperialism* (Oxford, UK: Oxford University Press, 2005), 137–82.

25. Cf. José Carlos Mariátegui, *Ni calque, ni copie*, anthology compiled and prefaced by Michael Löwy (Paris: Delga, 2020), 132.

26. Rosa Luxemburg, "Militarismus, Krieg und Arbeiterklasse: Rede vor der Frankfurter Strafkammer" [Militarism, war, and the working class: Speech to the Frankfurt criminal court] (February 22, 1914), *Ausgewählte Reden und Schriften*, vol. 2 (Berlin: Dietz Verlag, 1955), 499.

27. J. P. Nettl, *Rosa Luxemburg*, abridged ed. (London: Oxford University Press, 1969), 321–22.

28. Max Weber, "The Economic Foundations of 'Imperialism,'" quoted in Michael Löwy, *Max Weber et les paradoxes de la modernité* (Paris: PUF, 2012), 117–18.

29. Quoted in Paul Frölich, *Rosa Luxemburg, sa vie et son oeuvre* [Rosa Luxemburg: Her life and work] (Paris: Maspero, 1965), 263.

30. Nettl, *Rosa Luxemburg*, 373.

31. Julien Chuzeville and Eric Sevault, "Introduction," in Rosa Luxemburg, *La brochure de Junius, la guerre et l'Internationale (1907–1916)*, in *Oeuvres completes*, vol. 4, Julien Chuzeville, Marie Laigle, and Eric Sevault, eds. (Marseille and Toulouse: Agone/Smolny, 2014), xv. This document was published in Switzerland and signed with the pseudonym "Junius" (an eighteenth-century anti-monarchist pamphleteer).

32. Luxemburg, *Junius Pamphlet*, 193–97. Hannah Arendt suggested similar ideas in *The Origins of Totalitarianism*: European imperialism and colonialism are one of the primary sources of twentieth-century totalitarian regimes.

33. Luxemburg, *Junius Pamphlet*, 86. Cf. Rosa Luxemburg, "Junius", *Die Krise der Sozialdemokratie* (Bern: Unionsdruckerei, 1916), 11.

34. Luxemburg, *Junius Pamphlet*, 197.

35. Rosa Luxemburg, *Entweder–Oder* [Either-or] (1916), *Ausgewähtle Schriften*, vol. 2 (Berlin: Dietz Verlag, 1951), 533.

36. Nettl, *Rosa Luxemburg*, 408.

37. Luxemburg, *Entweder–Oder*, 543. These three figures were leaders of the right wing of the SPD, the majority, which supported the war policy of the imperial German government.

38. Luxemburg, *Entweder–Oder*, 542.

39. Luxemburg, *Entweder–Oder*, 542. Cf. Luxemburg, "Theses on the Tasks of International Social-Democracy," in *Junius Pamphlet*, 208.

40. Luxemburg, "Principes directeurs," 207.

41. Luxemburg, "Principes directeurs," 207.

42. Karl Liebknecht, "À Rosa Luxemburg: Remarques à propos du projet de theses pour le group 'Internationale'" [To Rosa Luxemburg—Remarks on her thesis project for the 'Internationale' group], *Partisans* 45 (January 1969), 113.

43. Luxemburg, "Principes directeurs," 209.

7. George Haupt, Internationalist
Under the Star of Rosa Luxemburg

1. Michael Löwy, "Georges Haupt, internationaliste" [Georges Haupt, internationalist], *Rouge*, April 1978, 16.

2. Claudie Weill, "Le séminaire de Georges Haupt à l'EHESS," *Le Mouvement Social* 111 (June 1980): 39–41.

3. Georges Haupt, Michel Lowy, Claudie Weill, *Les marxistes et la question nationale, 1848-1914* [Marxists and the national question] (Paris: Maspero, 1974).

4. Georges Haupt, *L'Historien et le mouvement social* [The historian and the social movement] (Paris: Maspero, 1980).

5. Quoted by Georges Haupt in his "Presentation" of Rosa Luxemburg, *Vive la lutte! Correspondance, 1891–1914*, (Paris: Maspero, 1975), 30.

8. Rosa Luxemburg and Trotsky

All quotations in this chapter cited to non-English sources translated by Lynne Sunderman.

1. Cf. Leon Trotsky, *Our Political Tasks* (1904) (New York: Oxford University Press, 1954), available at https://www.marxists.org/archive/trotsky/1904/tasks/.

2. Trotsky, in his last publication, *Stalin* (1940), declared that Lenin himself recognized the "one-sided, and therefore erroneous" theory exposed in *What Is to Be Done?* on the introduction of revolutionary consciousness "from outside" of the working class. Cf. Trotsky, *Stalin*, Charles Malamuth, ed. (New York: Stein & Day, 1967), 58.

3. Cf. Ernest Mandel, "The Leninist Theory of Organization," *International Socialist Review* (December 1970), available at https://www.marxists.org/archive/mandel/196x/leninism/index.htm.

4. Judging his own book *Our Political Tasks*, Trotsky in 1940 emphasized that it was "immature and erroneous" in its critique of Lenin, but that it nevertheless contained "a fairly accurate characterization of the cast

of thought of the 'committeemen' of those days, who have foregone the need to rely upon the workers after they had found support in the 'principles' of centralism."—the same committeemen who were the first embryo of the bureaucracy at the heart of the Bolshevik Party and whom Lenin found himself in constant struggle. Cf. Trotsky, *Stalin*, 62.

5. Rosa Luxemburg, "The Mass Strike, the Political Party, and the Trade Unions," in *Rosa Luxemburg Speaks*, Mary-Alice Waters, ed. (New York: Pathfinder, 1970), 203.

6. Cf. Trotsky, *The Permanent Revolution*, chap. 4. Cf., also, Leon Trotsky, *My Life* (New York: Pathfinder, 1970), 203: "At the London congress . . . on the question of the so-called permanent revolution, Rosa took the same stand that I did." In reality, however, on one crucial point, Rosa Luxemburg did not agree with Trotsky: for her, the Russian Revolution could never move beyond the democratic-bourgeois framework. For excellent coverage of this topic, see Norman Geras, *The Legacy of Rosa Luxemburg* (London: Verso, 1983).

7. Gilbert Badia, *Rosa Luxemburg, journaliste, polémiste, révolutionaire* [Rosa Luxemburg: journalist, polemicist, revolutionary] (Paris: Editions sociales, 1975), 337, 813.

8. André Glucksmann, "La Cuinière et le mangeur d'homes" [The cook and the cannibal], *le Seuil*, 1975, 106.

9. Daniel Singer, "C'est la faute à Karl Platon" [It's Karl Platon's fault], *Lire* 10, no. 18 (1976) 103–4.

10. Rosa Luxemburg, "The Russian Revolution," in *Rosa Luxemburg Speaks*, 375, 395.

11. Luxemburg, "The Russian Revolution," 389.

12. Luxemburg, "The Russian Revolution," 393.

13. Luxemburg, "The Russian Revolution," 394.

14. Ernest Mandel, "Dictatorship of the Proletariat and Socialist Democracy" (1977), position statement for the Fourth International, available at https://www.marxists.org/archive/mandel/1985/dictprole/1985.htm

9. Notes on Lukács and Rosa Luxemburg

All quotations in this chapter cited to non-English sources translated by Lynne Sunderman.

1. Georg Lukács, "Mein Weg zu Marx" [My road to Marx] (1933), in *Schriften zur Ideologie un Politik* (Luchterhand: Neuwied, 1967), 327.

2. See Michael Löwy, *Georg Lukács: From Romanticism to Bolshevism*

(New York: Schocken Books, 1979) on the relationship between revolutionary trade unionism and romantic anticapitalism, 41, 47–49.

3. Georg Lukács, *History and Class Consciousness* (Cambridge, MA: MIT Press, 1971), x.

4. Georg Lukács, "The Changing Function of Historical Materialism," in *History*, 237. This chapter is a significantly reworked version of a conference presentation from 1919. The passage quoted here appeared in the new edition from 1922.

5. Lukács, *History*, 37.

6. Lukács, *History*, 40.

7. Rosa Luxemburg, "The Mass Strike, the Political Party, and the Trade Unions," in *Rosa Luxemburg Speaks*, Mary-Alice Waters, ed. (New York: Pathfinder, 1970), 199.

8. Lukács, *History*, 41.

9. Luxemburg, "Mass Strike," 171.

10. Lukács, *History*, 41.

11. Lukács, *History*, 42.

12. Lukács, *History*, 45n15.

13. Georg Lukács, "Introduction to Rosa Luxemburg," in *Tämegsztrajk* [General strike] (Vienna: Verlag des Arbeiter-Buchhandlung, 1921), 3–9.

14. Georg Lukács, "Spontaneität der Massen, Aktivität der Partei" [Spontaneity of the masses, activity of the party], in *Werke*, vol. 2 (Neuwied: Luchterhand, 1968), 135.

15. Lukács, "Spontaneität," 136–37.

16. Lukács, "Spontaneität," 139.

17. Georg Lukács, "Organisatorische Fragen der revolutionären Initiative" [Organizational questions of revolutionary initiative], in *Werke*, vol. 2, 159.

18. Lukács, *History*, xli.

19. Lukács, *History*, 37.

20. Lukács, *History*, 298.

21. Lukács, *History*, 302–3.

22. Lukács, *History*, 298.

23. Lukács, *History*, 304.

24. Lukács, *History*, 307.

25. Lukács, *History*, 285, 304.

26. Lukács, *History*, 285.

27. Lukács, *History*, 316.

28. Lukács, *History*, 284.

29. Lukács, *History*, 317, 327; Lukács, *Histoire et Conscience de Classe* [History and class consciousness] (Paris: Minuit, 1960), 363, 373.

30. Lukács, *History*, 326, 332; Lukács, *Histoire et Conscience de Classe*, 372, 378

31. Lukács, *History*, 337.

32. Lukács, *History*, 336.

33. Lukács, *History*, 275.

34. Rosa Luxemburg, "Assemblée nationale ou gouvernement des conseils?" [National assembly or council government?], (1918) in *L'État bourgeois et la révolution* (Paris: La Breche, 1978), 45.

35. Rosa Luxemburg, *La Révolution russe* [The russian revolution] (Paris: Spartacus, 1946), 45–46. See also other English translations: "The Russian Revolution," in Waters, *Rosa Luxemburg Speaks*, and "On the Russian Revolution," in *The Complete Works of Rosa Luxemburg*, vol. 5, *Political Writings III, On Revolution 1910–1919*, Helen C. Scott and Paul Le Blanc, eds. (London: Verso, forthcoming).

36. Lukács, *History*, 291; György Lukács, *Geschichte und Klassenbewusstsein* [History and class consciousness] (Luchterhand: Neuwied, 1968), 468. (The French translation from Editions de Minuit here is poor.)

37. Luxemburg, "Russian Revolution" in *Rosa Luxemburg Speaks*, 393–94.

38. Luxemburg, *La Révolution russe*, 38–39.

39. Lukács, *History*, 292.

40. Lukács, *History*, 292.

41. Luxemburg, "Russian Revolution" in *Rosa Luxemburg Speaks*, 394

10. Ideology and Knowledge in Rosa Luxemburg

All quotations in this chapter cited to non-English sources translated by Lynne Sunderman.

1. Lelio Basso, "Introduzione," Rosa Luxemburg, *Lettere ai Kautsky* (E. Reuniti, 1971), 14.

2. Eduard Bernstein, "Entwicklungsgang eines Sozialisten" [Development of a socialist], in Felix Meiner, *Die Volkwirtschaftslehre der Gegenwart in Selbstdarstellungen* (Leipzig, 1924), 40. About Bernstein's philosophical ideas, Pierre Angel speaks of an "ethical positivism" inspired in part by Kant, Comte, and the liberal thinking of contemporary sociologists. Pierre Angel, *Eduard Bernstein et l'évolution du socialisme allemande* (Paris: Didier, 1961), 206.

3. On the debate on ethics, sociology, and socialism in this period, see the excellent essay by Lucien Goldmann, "Y a-t-il une sociologie marxiste?" [Is there a Marxist sociology?], in *Recherches dialectiques* (Paris: Gallimard, 1959).

4. Quoted in Victor Adler, *Briefwechsel mit August Bebel und Karl Kautsky* [Correspondence with August Bebel and Karl Kautsky], Friedrich Adler, ed. (Vienna: Verlag der Wiener Volksbuchhandlung, 1954), 259.

5. Eduard Bernstein, *Die Voraussetzungen des Sozialismus und die Aufgaben der Social-demokratie* [The prerequisites of socialism and the tasks of social democracy] (Stuttgart: J. H. W. Dietz, 1920), 25. The French translation (*Les présupposés du socialisme* [Paris: Seuil, 1974], 56) is here very poor. See English translation: *Evolutionary Socialism*, Edith Harvey, trans. (New York: Schocken, 1961).

6. Eduard Bernstein, *Les présupposés du socialisme* [Assumptions of socialism] (Paris: Seuil, 1974), 227.

7. Eduard Bernstein, *Wie ist der wissenschaftlichen Sozialismus möglich?* [How is scientific socialism possible?] (Berlin: Sozialistische Monatshefte, 1901), 20–35. Compare this with Durkheim, who explains that sociology "is neither individualist, communist, or socialist" and that "on principle, it disregards theories in which it finds no scientific value." *Les Règles de la méthode sociologique* [The rules of sociological method] (Paris: University Press of France, 1956), 140. It is no accident that Bernstein's article found favor with the French positivist economist Leroy-Beaulieu as noted in an article entitled, significantly, "L'Evolution du socialisme et la dissolution du socialisme scientifique" [The evolution of socialism and the dissolution of scientific socialism], *l'Economiste français* 51 (1901); cf. Angel, *Eduard Bernstein*, 300.

8. Basso, "Introduzione," 28. In 1875, before becoming Marxist, Kautsky had published a series of articles called "Darwin and Socialism" in the periodical *Volkstaat*. On the continuity of Kautsky's Darwinist problematic, see Erich Mathias, "Kautsky und der kautskyanismus" [Kautsky and Kautskyism], in *Marxismusstudien* (Tübingen: J. C. B. Mohr, 1957), 153.

9. Karl Kautsky, *Vermehrung und Entwicklung in Natur und Gesellschaft* [Reproduction and development in nature and society] (Stuttgart: Dietz, 1910), 11–12.

10. Karl Kautsky, *Erinnerungen und Erörterungen* [Memories and discussions] (The Hague: Mouton, 1960), 365.

11. Karl Kautsky, *Ethik und materialistische Geschichtsauffasung* [Ethics and the materialist conception of history] (1906), in *Marxismus und Ethik*, (Frankfurt: Suhrkamp, 1974), 258.

12. Kautsky, *Marxismus und Ethik*, 259. In the same vein from this period, see *Les Trois Sources du Marxisme* [The three sources of Marxism] (1907), in which Kautsky writes, "Knowledge that can be acquired

through the scientific system that Marx founded is out of reach to those who hold onto bourgeois society. Only he who is critical of bourgeois society, in other words, who puts himself in proletarian terrain, can attain this understanding. In this respect, proletarian science is distinct from bourgeois science." (Paris: Spartacus, 1969), 11.

13. Kautsky, *Marxismus und Ethik*, 259.

14. Karl Kautsky, *Die Materialistische Geschichtsauffassung* [The materialist conception of history], vol. 2 (Berlin: Dietz Verlag, 1927), 681. See English translation: Karl Kautsky, *The Materialist Conception of History*, Raymond Meyer with John H. Kautsky, trans., abridged ed. (New Haven, CT: Yale University Press, 1988).

15. Rudolf Hilferding, *Das Finanzkapital* (1910) (Berlin: Dietz, 1955), 3. See English translation: Rudolf Hilferding, *Finance Capital: A Study in the Latest Phase of Capitalist Development* (London: Routledge & Kegan Paul, 1985), available at https://www.marxists.org/archive/hilferding/1910/finkap/.

16. Max Adler, *Grundlegung der materialistischen Geschichtsauffassung* [Foundation of the materialist conception for history] (1930) (Vienna: Europa Verlag, 1964), 23–25. Max Adler's positions before 1914 were more nuanced; for him as for Kautsky, postwar writings revealed more positivist leanings.

17. Rosa Luxemburg, "Reform or Revolution," in *Rosa Luxemburg Speaks*, Mary-Alice Waters, ed. (New York: Pathfinder, 1970)

18. Rosa Luxemburg, *Introduction to Political Economy*, in *The Complete Works of Rosa Luxemburg*, vol. 1, *Economic Writings I*, Peter Hudis, ed. (London: Verso, 2016), 134.

19. Luxemburg, *Introduction to Political Economy*, 145.

20. Rosa Luxemburg, *The Accumulation of Capital: Introduction to Political Economy*, in *The Complete Works of Rosa Luxemburg*, vol. 2, *Economic Writings II*, Peter Hudis and Paul LeBlanc, eds. (London: Verso, 2016), 146.

21. Luxemburg, *Accumulation of Capital*, 471n164.

22. Luxemburg, *Accumulation of Capital*, 152, 228–29, 230, 471–72, 472n164.

23. Luxemburg, *Introduction to Political Economy*, 145.

24. Luxemburg, *Introduction to Political Economy*, 144.

25. Rosa Luxemburg, "Karl Marx" (1903), and "Stillstand und Fortschritt des Marxismus" [Stagnation and progress of Marxism" (1903), in *Gesammelte Werke*, vols. 1–2, (Berlin: Dietz Verlag, 1972), 367, 375. See English translation: "Stagnation and Progress of Marxism," in *Rosa*

Luxemburg Speaks, and "Marxist Theory and the Proletariat," available at https://www.marxists.org/archive/luxemburg/1903/03/14-abs.htm.

26. Rosa Luxemburg, "Aus dem literarischen Nachlass von Karl Marx," [From the literary estate of Karl Marx] (1905), in *Gesammelte Werke*, vols. 1–2, 469.

27. Cf. Rosa Luxemburg, *Réforme ou Révolution?*, 55; *Rosa Luxemburg Speaks*, 68: "What precisely was the key which enabled Marx to open the door to the secrets of capitalist phenomena and solve, as if in play, problems that were not even suspected by the greatest minds of classic bourgeois economy? It was his conception of capitalist economy as an historic phenomenon—not merely in the sense recognized in the best of cases by the classic economists, that is, when it concerns the feudal past of capitalism—but also in so far as it concerns the socialist future of the world. The secret of Marx's theory of value, of his analysis of the problem of money, of his theory of capital, of the theory of the rate of profit and consequently of the entire existing economic system is found in the transitory character of capitalist economy, the inevitability of its collapse leading—and this is only another aspect of the same phenomenon—to socialism. It is only because Marx looked at capitalism from the socialist's viewpoint, that is from the historic viewpoint, that he was enabled to decipher the hieroglyphics of capitalist economy. And it is precisely because he took the socialist viewpoint as a point of departure for his analysis of bourgeois society that he was in the position to give a scientific base to the socialist movement."

28. Luxemburg, "Stillstand und Fortschritt im Marxismus" [Stagnation and progress in Marxism], in *Gesammelte Werke*, vols. 1–2, 367. Rosa Luxemburg insists that this creative activity by the proletariat is practiced only in the field of *social* sciences.

29. Cf. Georg Lukács, *History and Class Consciousness* (Cambridge, MA: MIT Press, 1971).

30. Luxemburg, "Karl Marx," 377.

31. Luxemburg, *Réforme ou Révolution?*, 75. Our emphasis.

32. Antonio Gramsci, *El materialismo historico y la filosofia de Benedetto Croce* [Historical materialism and the philosophy of Benedetto Croce] (Buenos Aires: Lautaro, 1958), 98.

33. Louis Althusser, *Lire le Capital* [Reading *Capital*] (Paris: Maspero, 1965), 95. It is likely that Althusser would no longer defend the same ideas he had in 1965. See his *Éléments d'autocritique* [Elements of self-criticism] (Paris: Hachette, 1974).

Index

About the Authors

Michael Löwy is a French Brazilian Marxist sociologist and philosopher, and emeritus research director in social sciences at the National Centre for Scientific Research (CNRS) in Paris. His many books include *The Theory of Revolution in the Young Marx* and *On Changing the World*.

Paul Le Blanc, long-time activist and Professor of History at La Roche College, is the author of a number of widely-read studies, including *Lenin and the Revolutionary Party, From Marx to Gramsci*, and *Marx, Lenin and the Revolutionary Experience*. With Michael Yates he has written the widely acclaimed *A Freedom Budget for All Americans* and has coedited a selection of Leon Trotsky's *Writings in Exile*.

Helen C. Scott is Associate Professor of English at the University of Vermont. She is the editor of *Rosa Luxemburg: Socialism or Barbarism* (Pluto Press, 2010) and author of *Caribbean Women Writers and Globalization* (Routledge, 2006).

About Haymarket Books

Haymarket Books is a radical, independent, nonprofit book publisher based in Chicago. Our mission is to publish books that contribute to struggles for social and economic justice. We strive to make our books a vibrant and organic part of social movements and the education and development of a critical, engaged, and internationalist Left.

We take inspiration and courage from our namesakes, the Haymarket Martyrs, who gave their lives fighting for a better world. Their 1886 struggle for the eight-hour day—which gave us May Day, the international workers' holiday—reminds workers around the world that ordinary people can organize and struggle for their own liberation. These struggles—against oppression, exploitation, environmental devastation, and war—continue today across the globe.

Since our founding in 2001, Haymarket has published more than nine hundred titles. Radically independent, we seek to drive a wedge into the risk-averse world of corporate book publishing. Our authors include Angela Y. Davis, Arundhati Roy, Keeanga-Yamahtta Taylor, Eve L. Ewing, Aja Monet, Mariame Kaba, Naomi Klein, Rebecca Solnit, Olúfẹ́mi O. Táíwò, Mohammed El-Kurd, José Olivarez, Noam Chomsky, Winona LaDuke, Robyn Maynard, Leanne Betasamosake Simpson, Howard Zinn, Mike Davis, Marc Lamont Hill, Dave Zirin, Astra Taylor, and Amy Goodman, among many other leading writers of our time. We are also the trade publishers of the acclaimed Historical Materialism Book Series.

Haymarket also manages a vibrant community organizing and event space in Chicago, Haymarket House, the popular Haymarket Books Live event series and podcast, and the annual Socialism Conference.

Also Available from Haymarket Books

Ecosocialism: A Radical Alternative to Capitalist Catastrophe
Michael Löwy

The Essential Rosa Luxemburg: Reform or Revolution *and* The Mass Strike
Rosa Luxemburg, edited by Helen Scott

From Marx to Gramsci: A Reader in Revolutionary Marxist Politics
Edited by Paul Le Blanc

Lenin and the Revolutionary Party
Paul Le Blanc

Leon Trotsky and the Organizational Principles of the Revolutionary Party
Dianne Feeley, Paul Le Blanc, and Thomas Twiss, introduction by
George Breitman

The Living Flame: The Revolutionary Passion of Rosa Luxemburg
Paul Le Blanc

Marx in Paris, 1871: Jenny's "Blue Notebook"
Olivier Besancenot and Michael Löwy, translated by Todd Chretien

On Changing the World: Essays in Marxist Political Philosophy,
from Karl Marx to Walter Benjamin
Michael Löwy

The Politics of Combined and Uneven Development:
The Theory of Permanent Revolution
Michael Löwy

Revolutionary Collective:
Comrades, Critics, and Dynamics in the Struggle for Socialism
Paul Le Blanc

Revolutions
Michael Löwy

Rosa Luxemburg
Paul Frölich

Unfinished Leninism: The Rise and Return of a Revolutionary Doctrine
Paul Le Blanc

Printed in the USA
CPSIA information can be obtained
at www.ICGtesting.com
JSHW081538280124
56149JS00003B/4